D0477836

The publisher gratefully acknowledges the generous support of the August and Susan Frugé Endowment Fund in California Natural History of the University of California Press Foundation.

The publisher also gratefully acknowledges the generous support of the Director's Circle of the University of California Press Foundation, whose members are:

Anonymous
Wendy Ashmore
Janelle Cavanagh & Dominic Walshe
Earl & June Cheit
Charles R. & Mary Anne Cooper
Lloyd Cotsen
John & Jo De Luca
Sukey & Gilbert Garcetti / Roth Family Foundation
Walter S. Gibson
Harriett & Richard Gold
Prof. Mary-Jo DelVecchio Good & Prof. Byron Good
Gary K. Hart
Monica Heredia
Patricia & Robin Klaus
Watson M. & Sita Laetsch
Dr. Mary Gibbons Landor
David Littlejohn
Robert & Beverly Middlekauff
Lucinda Reinold
Lisa See & Richard Kendall
Ruth A. Solie
Judy & Bill Timken

In memoriam, the UC Press Foundation gratefully acknowledges the dedication and support of Diana P. Scott.

THE LEFT COAST

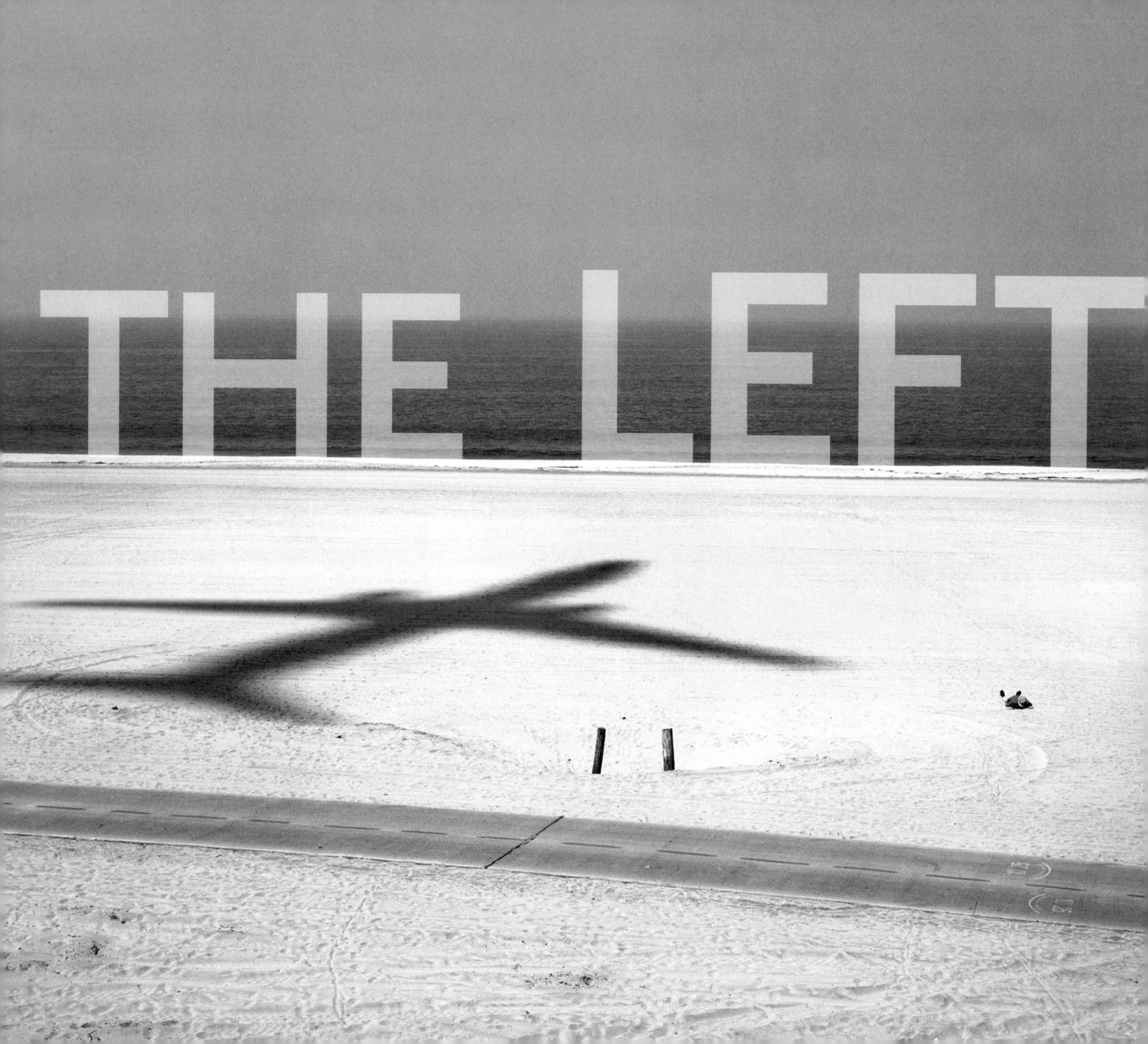
THE LEFT

COAST

CALIFORNIA ON THE EDGE

PHOTOS BY ALEX L. FRADKIN + TEXT BY PHILIP L. FRADKIN

UNIVERSITY OF CALIFORNIA PRESS | BERKELEY LOS ANGELES LONDON

University of California Press, one of the most distinguished university presses in the United States, enriches lives around the world by advancing scholarship in the humanities, social sciences, and natural sciences. Its activities are supported by the UC Press Foundation and by philanthropic contributions from individuals and institutions. For more information, visit www.ucpress.edu.

University of California Press
Berkeley and Los Angeles, California

University of California Press, Ltd.
London, England

Library of Congress Cataloging-in-Publication Data
Fradkin, Philip L.
    The left coast : California on the edge / text by Philip L. Fradkin ; photos by Alex L. Fradkin.
        p.   cm.
    Includes bibliographical references and index.
    ISBN 978-0-520-25509-8 (pbk. : alk. paper)
    1. California—Description and travel.   2. Coasts—California.   3. California—History.   4. Natural history—California.   5. Fradkin, Philip L.—Travel—California.
6. Fradkin, Alex (Alex Leon), 1966—Travel—California.
I. Fradkin, Alex (Alex Leon), 1966–.   II. Title.
    F866.2.F725   2011
    979.4—dc22   2010035056

Manufactured in China

20 19 18 17 16 15 14 13 12 11
10 9 8 7 6 5 4 3 2 1

The paper used in this publication meets the minimum requirements of ANSI/NISO Z39.48–1992 (R 1997) (*Permanence of Paper*).

To Dad, for the first time

For Alex, again

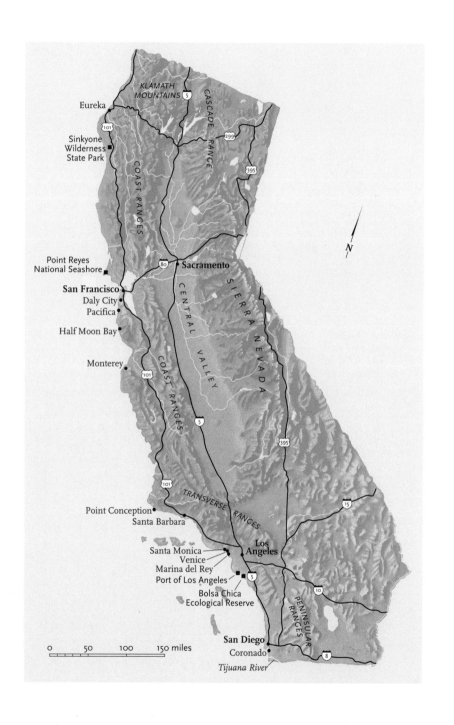

KLAMATH
MOUNTAINS

Eureka

Sinkyone
Wilderness
State Park

CASCADE RANGE

COAST RANGES

Point Reyes
National Seashore

Sacramento

San Francisco
Daly City
Pacifica

CENTRAL VALLEY

SIERRA NEVADA

Half Moon Bay

Monterey

COAST RANGES

Point Conception
Santa Barbara

TRANSVERSE RANGES

Santa Monica
Venice
Marina del Rey
Port of Los Angeles
Bolsa Chica
Ecological Reserve

Los
Angeles

PENINSULAR RANGES

San Diego
Coronado

Tijuana River

0   50   100   150 miles

N

CONTENTS

PROLOGUE

viii

Until I began working on this book, I didn't realize to what extent I was an aqueous person. True, I'm a Pisces, but by *aqueous* I mean I'm intensely drawn to salt water. Freshwater just won't do it. It's too thin. It knifes through my nostrils like cold air, leaving a momentary sting. Salt water is thick and pungent with the smells of distant continents and a blended decay that bespeaks an abundance of life-forms. There have been just a few years—I view them as involuntary exile—when I haven't lived, worked, or played near salt water, whether on the south shore of Long Island in New York State or in the coastal counties of Marin and Los Angeles in California.

Language and physical features separate the two edges of the continent. In the East it is "the shore," meaning the Jersey shore or the north and south shores of Long Island. *Shore* is a sibilant word that fits long, flat stretches of sandy beaches lapped by soft, hissing surf. In eastern publications, "the

Coast" is a synonym for the western edge of the continent and an ambiguous portion of the whole state. The abruptness of the word matches the steep bluffs and rocky headlands that provide so much drama in Northern California. South of Point Conception, the more prevalent use of the word *beach* indicates a softening of the interface between salt water and land in Southern California. Orientation to a map provides yet another viewpoint, with its own set of echoes. *Left,* as in *The Left Coast,* denotes someone or something that is different, strange, a bit noir, or liberal.

As for my attraction to and the magnetic pull of salt water upon me, the facile explanation is the astrological sign under which I was born. For some people that explanation will suffice. For the more seriously inclined, there is no easy explanation, other than what may be known about inherited characteristics and early influences of a landscape upon an individual.

Deserts, mountains, valleys, canyons, and prairies affect others in similar ways. Actually, all those places in the American West draw me, but none as powerfully as the coast.

In my search for the essence of the California coast and a suitable description for others who may not be as deeply involved in it as I have been for the last fifty years, I have divided the coastline according to eight major uses or activities and assigned them chapters. For each function I have selected an emblematic place to illustrate it. The eight coasts of California and the places whose particular uses I have chosen to describe are "The Wild Coast" (Sinkyone Wilderness), "The Agricultural Coast" (western Marin County), "The Residential Coast" (Daly City, Pacifica, Half Moon Bay), "The Tourist Coast" (Monterey), "The Recreational Coast" (Santa Monica, Venice, Marina del Rey), "The Industrial Coast" (Port of Los Angeles), and "The Military Coast" (San Diego). "The Political Coast" (Bolsa Chica Ecological Reserve) is an example of how a law and its political implementation have shaped the continent's western edge.

The quotes at the beginning of each chapter provide insights of others from the past, thus contributing to and deepening the inquiry. The photographs illustrate the different activities but range more widely than my descriptions to give the subject a greater geographic and interpretive reach. Combined, the words and images not only define the coast, but they also go a long way toward explaining California. The coast, in many ways, *is* California, for most of the state's population lives within its narrow strip.

I am not a disinterested observer. My memories are included in this account because they explain my interest in coastal matters, contain some history, and form a cycle dating back to my first book, *California: The Golden Coast,* published in 1974. They also provide a human perspective by describing, in part, a father-son relationship. My then-young son, Alex, accompanied me on my research trips for that book. My now-middle-aged son took the photographs for this book and did much of the driving. The first coast book was dedicated to him, as is this book—thus the cycle is completed as I approach old age. We are partners in this second coastal venture, the only difference being our means of expression and the specific tools we use to communicate our messages. I think we are fairly close in terms of tone and intent.

The reader will notice that the photographs don't follow the structural device I chose to portray the coast. We began this project thinking there should be a close relationship, and then we both felt constrained by the artificiality of tying the photos directly to the text. The images range geographically and topically further from, but still relate to, the eight categories. They flow more freely in accordance with their greater artistic expressiveness that demanded their own associative arrangements. We believe the book comes closer than any previous work to capturing the shadings and extremes of coastal complexities. We have done this by combining personal, historic, journalistic, autobiographical, and artistic components into both a literal and an emblematic document. (Alex has more to say about his photographs in his essay at the end of this book.)

When I wrote my two coastal books, I thought the politics of coastal protection were as important as the places themselves. Thus, I address the politics in the last chapters of both works. But the politics of coastal land use are but a dot within the vast stretch of geologic time that will eventually erase our momentary footprints from the sandy beaches where tides continuously come and go.

A cycle in my life has been completed with this book. I can now say good-bye to the totality of the California coast and concentrate on enjoying the one small place where I have lived for more than thirty years on the shoreline of a bay. I hope readers will be able to determine from this book what attracts them to the western littoral and then do something to protect its essential nature. Passing on the torch of coastal concern is one of my goals in writing this book, just as receiving that flame in the early 1970s was an obligation.

COASTAL MEMORIES

I began my salt-water-oriented life in the pre–World War II years on the south shore of Long Island, where my family had a summer house. The half-day automobile journey began on a hillside in Montclair, New Jersey; progressed through or around the tip of Manhattan; and finally ended on the flat terminal moraine of Long Island in the small farm community and summer colony of East Quogue, which straddled Montauk Highway seventy-five miles east of New York City. East Quogue was an ordinary place set among the various Hamptons. My family owned ten acres, nine of them rented to a farmer. A duck farm was on the far side of the property, bordering a creek. When the wind was right, the smell was ripe. My father, who had been raised on a large estate in Russia, created a much smaller version on Long Island. Potatoes were raised on both properties. In Russia they were used to make vodka, and in Long Island they were sold by the farmer or gathered by us to be

eaten. The farm has since become a subdivision and the creek was dredged to accommodate docks and boats.

Beyond our street lay Shinnecock Bay, and beyond the bay there was a narrow barrier beach and sand dunes that softened the onslaught of the Atlantic Ocean during the hurricane season. We periodically headed back to New Jersey before such storms, one being the destructive 1938 hurricane that breached the spit, forming Shinnecock Inlet. The narrow defile carved by the hurricane was my first memory of the power of moving salt water. The consequences of hurricanes have proven to me that people on the East Coast are no wiser than those on the West Coast. A family friend who was to become my brother-in-law was rescued from the second floor of his home in Westhampton Beach in 1938. While he was married to my sister, a home he built on stilts on the barrier beach was destroyed by a later hurricane. New homes have risen in the same location, just as new homes rise on fire-scarred coastal hillsides in California.

When I was a small boy during the war, the ocean beach was a safe place to play while others died on more distant shores. A roped rectangle with painted barrels defined the swimming area guarded by lifeguards. There were bathhouses, freshwater showers, and food at the private beach clubs. There was also my mother's command to wait an unbearable length of time after eating before going back into the water. I rode the waves on an inflated rubber mattress—surfing, East Coast style. It was, as I look back, a privileged life of almost constant pleasures lasting into my late teens. The only discordant note was the polio that struck two players on my baseball team. I was hustled back to New Jersey with the same dispatch employed to escape oncoming hurricanes.

The West Coast differed from what I expected. At my first encounter with the Pacific Ocean, I was quickly disabused of the myth of scantily attired young women lolling near warm water. I aimed my Volkswagen bug loaded with all my worldly possessions through the summer heat of Death Valley, over Tioga Pass, and into Yosemite National Park in 1960. I crossed the San Joaquin Valley and the Coast Range and sped down Highway 1 to Big Sur. I turned right onto a dirt road. After paying a nominal toll to the farmer, whose property I had to cross, I parked at Pfeiffer Beach.

Trailing the stink of sweat and dirt accumulated on the five-day, cross-country journey, I ran straight toward the inviting ocean and plunged into the surf, just as I would have done on Long Island. The frigid water was my first exposure to the deceptive nature of the West Coast. I encountered the second when I surfaced to confront the black-masked face and two unblinking eyes of a sea lion staring directly at me. I tried to make my way back to the beach, but I was pulled seaward. I swam sideways to the riptide, managed to get my frozen feet onto the sandy bottom, and stumbled to the white, sun-warmed sand, where I collapsed, depleted and badly frightened.

I had come seeking my first newspaper job, and eventually I found it at a small weekly south of San Francisco in a city bordering the saltwater marsh that edged the bay in San Mateo County. It was a period of great growth, and the shoreline of San Francisco Bay was being filled with developments. A few people became alarmed, and they began a "save the bay" campaign that resulted in the formation of the Bay Area Conservation and Development Commission, the model for the later coast commissions. I remained in San Carlos for six months, then moved inland.

After a two-year exile from the coast spent in the San Joaquin Valley town of Turlock, I returned to the Bay Area in 1962, where I was married. My wife and I lived among the houseboats on the shoreline of Richardson Bay in Sausalito. We had a sailboat that took us to Sam's Anchor Café in Tiburon, to Angel Island, and into the Sacramento–San Joaquin river deltas. It was here, while working for the Marin County newspaper, that I first encountered a sustained effort to protect the coast. I wrote about a proposed nuclear power plant near Bodega and logging and subdivision developments on the Point Reyes Peninsula. I visited its small county beaches.

Access to the remainder of the peninsula was blocked by private property. The conservationists pushed for a pristine national seashore. The ranchers resisted, saying they belonged there too. There was a workable compromise. Part of the national seashore was deemed worthy of official wilderness designation, another part was set aside for ranching. Something endangered and of value had been saved in both instances. Preservation was a minor goal then. The goal of most Californians in those years, which seems silly now, was to exceed the population of New York, then the nation's most populous state.

In 1964 I went from sleepy Marin County to teeming Los Angeles and a large metropolitan newspaper. I made the coastal transition in a twenty-two-foot, gaff-rigged, topsail cutter with hard chimes, a concrete keel, a long bowsprit, and the graceful lines of a Monterey Bay fishing boat. My wife and I passed Point Conception, that stormy protrusion dividing Northern and Southern California, on a windless, clear, early fall night under the power of a small diesel engine. Lights twinkled kindly on shore.

That sailboat and a leased acre of land on a rocky point south of Ensenada in Baja California, Mexico, were what kept me sane during racial conflicts, wildfires, floods, assassinations, student unrest, war in South Vietnam, and antiwar riots. It was my job at the *Los Angeles Times* to record most of this turmoil. Weekends I sailed to peaceful Catalina Island or drove to Mexico and camped on the rocky, wave-buffeted point. Increasingly, I made those journeys alone, or I took my young son, Alex.

My wife and I separated in 1970, after I returned from a stint as a correspondent in South Vietnam. I sought a place to heal by the ocean and found an affordable apartment overlooking Cabrillo Beach in the Point Fermin area of San Pedro. After work, I went bodysurfing or walked along the pier and watched people fish for food, not sport. The beach was well used by the residents of South Central Los Angeles, particularly on weekends. The sounds of music and the smells of barbecue filled the air.

What I found on that beach and elsewhere along the California coast as the first environmental writer for the *Times* was an intense competition for space that was being won by developers and public agencies with outsized plans. Little was being done to plan the coast wisely and then implement that plan with meaningful controls. The state legislature failed repeatedly to pass coastal protection bills. So "Save the coast" became the rallying cry for an initiative measure, known as Proposition 20, on the November 1972 ballot. The initiative set up one statewide and six regional commissions with permit powers to rule on coastal projects while a plan was being formulated. It was heavily weighted toward maintaining the status quo, virtually unheard of previously as a land use policy in California.

It is difficult now, given the hundreds of initiative measures that have since been on California ballots, to appreciate how unusual Proposition 20 was at the time. First of all, the signatures necessary for placing it on the ballot were gathered by volunteers, not disinterested paid help. Second, an initiative measure, especially one successfully formulated outside the confines of state government, was not the way to pass laws at that time. On the one side were the seemingly unstoppable land developers with subdivisions and condominiums and hotels, oil companies with oil platforms and onshore processing facilities, and utility firms with coal and nuclear power plants on their drawing boards. On the other was a loose, fractious coalition of big and little environmental groups. It was David versus Goliath, with certain advantages for the former. Saving the coast, as opposed to winning a difficult war, was a popular issue following the 1969 Santa Barbara oil spill and the first Earth Day the next year. It made people feel righteous. "If you were against the initiative," I wrote at the time, "you couldn't say 'destroy our coast.' The arguments had to be more complex and thus elusive."[1]

The lack of public access to the coastline personalized the issue. Almost everyone who didn't live directly on the coast had his or her story about being blocked from the beach. One story I wrote for the *Times* concerning access still sticks in my mind. It wasn't a front-page story. It sat, almost inconspicuously, inside the Metro section and contained what I thought was the minor revelation that Los Angeles County had done nothing to open new or enforce existing public access paths to the Malibu beach. The phone calls and mail I received from outraged Malibu residents, who wanted to protect their special enclave from outsiders, surpassed in quantity and vitriol the responses I received to more significant stories.

The *Times'* endorsement of Proposition 20 was crucial because, while Northern California was more conservation-minded and could be counted on to support it, the vast bulk of voters resided in Southern California. The powerful newspaper was the only unifying media presence in Southern California. Tony Day, the editor of the editorial pages, called me to his office on the second floor and grilled me on the initiative. I said it was carefully written, was not radical in approach, and would be effective in the right ways. The Chandler family, who owned the *Times,* had a lot of coastal real estate. But the publisher, Otis Chandler, was an active surfer who had heard from less-affluent surfers about their lack of access to beaches. The editorial board, with Chandler present, considered the matter. The paper endorsed Proposition 20, which won handily by a 55 percent majority.

The commissions had three years to formulate a plan and become established as a permanent governmental entity by the legislature and the governor. I covered the commissions during their first two years. I was also a beneficiary of their deliberations. The City of Los Angeles, through its powerful Department of Recreation and Parks, wanted to build the Cabrillo Marine Aquarium at the north end of the sandy beach on Point Fermin. That meant cutting down trees, displacing valuable beach space, and locating the building adjacent to the tide pools in the much-picked-over Point Fermin Marine Life Refuge. The aquarium would be immediately under the fragile, fossil-rich sandstone cliff on which the four-unit apartment complex in which I lived was precariously perched. What subsequent beach erosion, the effects of global warning, and fierce El Niño–bred storms might have done to the structure was given no consideration.

The Department of Recreation and Parks got its plan through the regional coast commission without any Point Fermin residents being aware of it, let alone opposed to it. City crews began preparing to cut down the trees on Washington's Birthday, and I gave up and left in disgust for the day. When I returned in the late afternoon, the trees were still standing and younger surfers, swimmers, and sunseekers who used the beach during the week were perched on the branches. There was a standoff. Chain saws idled ominously, and the police stood by. I called my friends in the news departments of television stations. They arrived with camera crews, and we crucified the city on the birthday of the president who said he couldn't tell a lie.

My next-door neighbor was a lawyer, and we two older men joined forces. I appeared before the Recreation and Parks Commission, while he dealt with the legal issues. We recruited a politically ambitious Westside lawyer, who got the coast commission to reverse its position and require that the aquarium be built off the beach and on what was then a paved parking lot. In 2008 I talked with the director of the aquarium, and he thanked me for what we had done. Not only had it allowed the structure to survive natural disasters, but it had also enabled it to expand in the larger space, he said.

About this time I began work on my first book. Six-year-old Alex joined me on a research trip to the North Coast in 1972. We traveled back roads, camped in a tent at night, and cooked our dinner over a one-burner backpacking stove. Our staple was Top Ramen mixed with anything that was handy. To begin the trip, I drove straight to the Oregon border, and we stopped at Pelican Beach, "where a child's imagination runs wild and an adult seeks meaning in forms and comfort in texture," I subsequently wrote. We then headed south and camped on Gold Bluffs Beach

in Prairie Creek State Park. "Two bull Roosevelt elk engaged in a stylized combat. We remained silent—no small feat for my son—as we continued to eat our dinner." At the mouth of the Mattole River, we encountered a man who introduced himself simply as Dan. Dan lived in a driftwood shelter and charmed Alex by showing him his mongrel named Stony and letting him handle the dog's nine puppies. We continued down the coast collecting material for *California: The Golden Coast*. It was published in 1974.

I soon found myself bumping up against the limits of daily journalism. Jerry Brown was elected governor, and some environmentalists I knew had joined his administration in 1975. I was offered and took a job as assistant secretary of the California Resources Agency, which was in charge of the departments that dealt with environmental matters. I was responsible for overseeing public affairs, energy, and coastal matters. My goal was to make the coast commission permanent. But since the unspoken policy within the Brown administration was "No personal agendas!" I had to be careful, and Machiavellian, in my approach.

The departments within the agency opposed any infringements on their turf, and the coast commissions usurped many of their responsibilities. I quickly hit upon the strategy of representing the departments' positions forcefully and accurately, thinking correctly that the self-serving nature of their objections would work in favor of the proposed coast commission. It did, but it also brought me condemnation by my conservationist friends. The climactic meeting to determine the Brown administration's policy took place in the governor's office. Gray Davis, Brown's chief of staff who would become governor in 1999, chaired the meeting. The departments' objections were duly noted with little enthusiasm. Other politics of the moment were the dominant concern: Brown had embarked on his first unsuccessful campaign for the Democratic presidential nomination and wanted to fly to Oregon the next day and endorse the pending California coastal legislation in that land-use-conscious state. He did, and meaningful coastal legislation passed in 1976.

I left state government shortly afterward to go to work as *Audubon* magazine's first western editor, and moved to the Point Reyes Peninsula. It was, for me, nirvana. I was encircled by every type of salt-water landscape imaginable: open ocean, bays, estuaries, wetlands, deltas, sandy beaches, islets, islands, rocky headlands, coastal hills, and a picturesque lighthouse perched dramatically at the end of a point. Almost all the terrain was in either national or state park systems. Restrictive zoning ordinances, strict building codes, agricultural easements, and a unified community protected the remainder.

We were, and are, a California anomaly: a community dedicated to preserving, not developing, and to keeping change to a minimum. We believe small, slow, and local are beneficial. Along those lines, we have vetoed sewers and depend upon septic systems, we don't seek water supplies beyond our immediate surroundings, we raise some of the food we eat, and we think of ourselves as bounded by watersheds and not artificial boundaries. We are liberal, Democratic, and fairly affluent. When we leave, we go "over the hill" to east Marin, a phrase that implies a geographical and cultural divide.

We are situated, however, within a wider context. The California coast stretches eleven hundred miles from the Oregon state line to the Mexican border; or, to put it in terms more expressive of its great latitudinal reach, from a dense, dripping rain forest to an open, scratchy desert. The equivalent distances in the Midwest are from Cincinnati to New Orleans and in the East from Boston to the border of the Carolinas. The coast is long; in fact, it is very long and thus very diverse. Along the way there are extremes in the types of natural beauty, human despoliation, and the occupations and constructs of humans that mirror what occur elsewhere in California.

Human tides of immigrants and migrants have repeatedly swept over the coast. First came the earliest Native Americans migrating via the Bering Strait land bridge from the north. They were succeeded by the tribes who pushed their predecessors out. Then the Spanish arrived from the south. They were followed by the Anglo-dominated races from the east during the Gold Rush years. Asian-dominated races arrived before and after the turn of the nineteenth century from the west. Most recently Latinos, again from the south, and Asians, again from the west, have arrived on the shores of California. There were lesser ebbs and flows of populations in between these major inundations. The result is a human history dominated by rapid change and transience and a varied landscape that no one group could lay claim to for an extensive length of time, although each succeeding cluster has made that attempt.

All eventually became Californians, and Californians are irresistibly drawn to water. They want to see, smell, touch, bathe, and surf in it, or just be in its presence, whether supine, sitting, standing, or camping. There is a herd instinct at work here. The long oceanic swells that cross the Pacific in one direction clash with the human tides, including millions of tourists each year, who migrate westward toward the narrow coastal strip. People move in and occupy this tightly packed land base, pushing others closer to the edge until, quite literally, they topple in their ill-conceived dwellings into the ocean that continuously eats away at the land. A compacted human mass clings precariously to the earthquake-, storm-, and wildfire-riddled coast, where the climate is equitable, the living gracious, and the scenery spectacular. What I wrote years ago is still true: "Everyone in the nation's most populous state wants a piece of the coastline."[2]

The road passed through a region of prosperous farms, and gradually approached the coast, which here is not high, though backed by broken ground that rises to the dignity of hills. Blocks of dark timber diversified the landscape, and the shore was picturesquely varied with storm-blown spruces and a foam-ringed islet or two. I gazed with particular interest at the northward reaches of the coast, for though there was nothing notable in the view, I realized that at last I was looking up the coast at Oregon. **J. Smeaton Chase, 1911**

THE WILD COAST

Between Cape Vizcaino and Point Delgada are several small, exposed landings available for use only in the summer and in smooth weather. These landings ship ties, tan bark, and shingles, and then only when they can be handled at a profit; and the landings are abandoned or revived according to commercial demands. Wire cables are used in loading and discharging, mooring buoys being placed where necessary. Supplies are not obtainable and communication is irregular. The principal landings are Rockport, Monroe landing, Usal, Bear Harbor, and Needle Rock. **United States Coast Pilot, 1909**

The world [*né*] is flat. There was a flood because of man's wickedness. One man, Nagaicho, flattened the world when he made it over. He had tall timber and jumped on top of it until the water went down. He studied what to do then. He went to the ocean and worked and patched up the banks and opened the rivers quickly. Then he planted plants and bushes. He made everything easy for man. Man is the one who makes it hard for himself because he does so much wrong. **"The Flood," a creation story told by Jack Woodman, a Sinkyone Indian, to Gladys Ayer Nomland, 1935**

For nearly three decades after American occupation of California, "Indian wars" continued—the Klamath War of 1851–52, Kern River War of 1856, Pit River massacres of 1867, and the Modoc War of 1873. During the campaign of 1855–59 in the north, soldiers killed more than 100 Indians, while settlers of the Mad and Eel River regions put at least 200 to death in a series of massacres. *The WPA Guide to California*, **1939**

There is no seven-foot barrier, no armed patrols backed by the technical wizardry of modern warfare directed against guerilla movements, no dense toxic sludge that breeds diseases at the northernmost coastal portal into the state of California. Those physical impediments are at the very southern end of the narrow coastal strip. The differences between Oregon and California are far more subtle and less dramatic than those between California and Mexico. Take, for example, the two units of the state park systems of Oregon and California that straddle the border within a quarter mile of each other.

The short road into the Oregon park on the north side of the Winchuck River, where it empties into the ocean, is carefully graded and neatly delineated by boulders. Just south of the California Agricultural Inspection Station, there is a sharp turn to the ocean. The road into Pelican Beach State Park is pockmarked by deep potholes, dusty, and littered with trash and discarded household items, including a table and rug. It is used, in other words, as a dump. What this tells me is that Oregon has managed to maintain an orderly presence, while the Golden State has lapsed into disrepair.

I have clear memories of sitting here on Pelican Beach on a warm, early fall day and watching Alex climb over the weathered driftwood logs and play in the sand. In this land of nearly perpetual fog or rain, I have somehow had the luck to return on the same type of day, when there is, and was, "an aching intensity of light and color."[1] The same restaurant, slightly enlarged, still stands just to the south, but the modular cottages stained a redwood color, which can be rented or purchased, are new. *Oceanview* and *oceanfront* are the words used most frequently to advertise dining, sleeping, residential, and commercial attractions. The words are scattered along the roadside for a few miles beyond the Tolowa Indian gaming casino, up to the point where Highway 101 bends inland.

I stopped at the inspection station to find out who was entering California and what they were bringing with them. Al Mikkelsen was on the lookout for western fruit flies in cherries, gypsy moths in webs spun on the underside of recreational vehicles, tan oak that might be harboring sudden oak death, exotic Quaker parrots, and various other noxious items. In the summer months he checks between twenty-five hundred and three thousand vehicles during an eight-hour shift. In winter, there are one-third that number.

Many of the people passing through are locals who live in nearby Brookings, Oregon. Quite a few of the locals work at the Lucky 7 Casino or Pelican Bay State Prison, which is inland and south of the bay whose name was appropriated by California's most notorious supermax prison. The back road that leads to the prison has an unusual number of small cafés advertising espresso coffee. I can only guess the guards need to get jacked up before going to work. Mikkelsen also lives in Brookings, where state taxes are lower, the annual vehicle registration fee is only fifty-two dollars, and gas, which is by law dispensed by an attendant, is forty cents less a gallon than in California.

Mikkelsen's questioning of border crossers went something like this:

"Hi there. Any fresh fruit on board?"

"No."

"Have a good day."

And, easy as that, the visitor was in California.

South of Ferndale and Petrolia on the narrow coastal road, and west of Redway and Garberville on the 101 freeway, is the Lost Coast, the wildest and least-trafficked section of the California shoreline. There are no roads or railroads along the coast here, as there are elsewhere. Three roads provide access at points at the north, middle, and south end of the fifty-six-mile stretch of shoreline that extends from the mouth of the Mattole River to Usal Creek. Except for the Shelter Cove subdivision in the middle of the wilderness, the Lost Coast is protected. It is divided into the King Range National Conservation Area on the north and the much smaller Sinkyone Wilderness State Park on the south.

Steep mountains, grassy meadows, and thick forests tumble downward to meet the metric beat of the relentless ocean waves upon the rocky shoreline. But the Lost Coast is neither lost nor wild in the strictest senses of those words. Its name was applied in the 1930s, when many of its inhabitants fled during one of the periodic logging depressions. This stretch of coast has since been repopulated by visitors who like to hike, fish, and surf. The long airstrip at Shelter Cove was once used by small commercial airliners to transport prospective lot purchasers back and forth from Southern California. There is a smaller landing strip serving a remote campground also reachable by hikers on the coastal trail and by high-speed motorboats carrying surfers and campers who do not wish to lug heavy backpacks across sand and rocks. Inland, the main crop is marijuana, which represents somewhere between 25 and 75 percent of the local economy, precise measurements being impossible to determine because of the illegal nature of the crop. It's best to heed the numerous "No trespassing" signs.

This is a land of geologic and climactic extremes. There are frequent earthquakes caused by the nearby meeting of three tectonic plates, 150 inches of yearly rainfall, 16 inches of rain from a single storm, landslides thundering down steep four-thousand-foot hillsides, hot summer days exceeding one hundred degrees, and cool summer fog two hundred miles north of the urban comforts of San Francisco.

The natural and human histories of the coast begin here with the coast redwood trees and the Sinkyone Indians, whose stories are intertwined and parallel each other. They represent the tales of other endemic species and Native Americans in California. Both were abundant, both were nearly eradicated, and the populations of both have stabilized if not increased in recent years. Their histories can be told through the stories of three virgin redwood groves and a second-growth Douglas fir and tan oak forest in the Sinkyone Wilderness section of the Lost Coast.

The range of the redwood tree, more formally known as *Sequoia sempervirens,* extends from just above the Oregon border to southern Monterey County in the midsection of the state. The redwood is extreme in terms of grace, majesty, spirituality, age, and height. The world's tallest living tree is a redwood that reaches the height of 379 feet. These übertrees have attracted more tourists and local visitors to ancient redwood groves in state and national parks than any other arboreal destinations in the state. The roadside attractiveness of redwoods is so great that the coastal region north of San Francisco is known as the Redwood Empire.

The fossil record indicates that the redwood genus of trees *(Sequoia)* has existed for as long as 240 million years, meaning as far back as the age of the dinosaurs. The trees once circled the globe in the temperate midlatitudes. A *sempervirens* variety was present in the Rocky Mountain states 60 million years ago. The tree migrated westward to southern California 40 million years ago, escaping extreme summer and winter temperatures. As southern California became warmer during the Pleistocene period, the redwoods' range narrowed to their present humid coastal niche in central and northern California. The drip of frequent coastal fogs adds between 25 and 50 percent to the annual rainfall, which in itself is no small amount.

About 8,000 years ago, humans arrived where redwoods grew. Some of the oldest redwood trees alive today predate the birth of Christ by approximately 200 years. Middle-age trees were seedlings during the medieval warm period, 600 to 900 years ago. Younger redwoods date back to the little ice age, 150 to 350 years ago, proving climate change is a constant.

It took only sixty years to seriously deplete the old-growth redwood forest. Steam- and gas-fed engines, the post–World War II housing boom, and the boutique use of redwood greatly hastened its near demise. The wood was coveted for its fire-resistant quality, resistance to rot, lack of shrinkage, and attractive reddish grain when freshly cut, and gray weathered patina when aged. It was also cheap, at least initially, because of its abundance. Redwood was used for the exterior walls of offices, homes, barns, and shacks and to make grape stakes, shingles, shakes, wine vats, water tanks, hot tubs, water flumes, floodgates, bridges, trestles, wharf pilings, furniture, fences, and coffins.

From the excesses of the Victorian mansions in redwoodland to the starkness of the mining-camp-inspired architecture of modern Sea Ranch on the Sonoma coast to the Bernard Maybeck–inspired California bungalows in the San Francisco Bay Area, redwood was the tree of choice. From around 1900 to the 1960s, the world knew redwood in abundance. Then the decline began, leaving the spare remains of logging settlements scattered along the coast of the Sinkyone Wilderness and elsewhere in Northern California. These remnant workplaces and habitations have become almost invisible after only fifty years, which is a tribute to the fecundity of the landscape. They are stark reminders of the fleeting presence of humans upon a landscape belonging to no one except the particular animal species or human group living upon it during a passing moment in time.

Drive south from Ferndale or west from Garberville, and the paved road becomes narrower and more circuitous and the evidence of human habitation more rare, until finally the road descends steeply and becomes a narrow dirt track accommodating one vehicle with a few turnoffs for oncoming traffic. A few bumpy miles later, it ends in what was once an orchard. Bear Harbor is less than a half-mile walk to the south. A retaining wall and a few domestic plants that have survived in the wild are the only signs of what was once a throbbing logging enterprise.

A great future had once been foreseen for Bear Harbor. A member of an exclusive San Francisco hunting club who was traveling the coast in 1857 commented on the possibilities of the harbor: "Taking into view the remarkable progress of California, it certainly is not anticipating too much to look forward to the day when Bear Harbor will be a great emporium of commerce and industry."[2] White settlers followed Sinkyone Indian footpaths into the Lost Coast area in the early 1860s, when the land was opened to homesteading as the Civil War raged far to the east. The Humboldt Trail was cut along the ridgeline to the east of Bear Harbor. It carried foot, horse, and mule traffic up and down the coast from Eureka to Fort Bragg, with a westward branch to Bear Harbor and nearby Needle Rock established in 1865.

Sheltered from the prevailing northwest winds by rocks off a minuscule point, but not from storms from the south, landings from sailing ships were first made on the black sand beach. Redwood railroad ties, posts, shingles, and profitable tan oak bark, from which tannic acid could be extracted, were transported to the tossing offshore vessels. The acid was used to process leather goods in forty California tanneries. A new process was found. Tan oaks are now considered a trash tree susceptible to sudden oak disease.

Orchards were planted in meadows where live-

stock grazed. Ranch houses and line camps clung to hillsides or found a bit of flat space in the narrow canyons. It was a precarious and extremely remote life, particularly in the wet winter months, but at least there was a bare living to be made as long as the trees lasted. The harvesting of timber intensified when Bear Harbor became the center of regional logging activity near the end of the century. Money, machines, and the inventiveness and persistence of humans under extremely harsh conditions made it possible. A five-hundred-foot wharf with pilings inserted into holes drilled into offshore rocks housed a steam-driven donkey engine that drove a cable used to load and off-load cargo from ships anchored three hundred feet beyond the end of the wharf.

A badly degraded Railroad Creek flowed through the narrow canyon that flared into what was once a small coastal marsh at Bear Harbor. In the canyon and spilling onto the former marsh were sheds, residences, bunkhouses, a schoolhouse, stacked lumber products, and a railroad. More than one thousand feet of vertical rails connected the landing with what was then the Humboldt Trail and is now the Usal Road at the six-hundred-foot level of Jackass Ridge. Gravity, horses, and propulsion furnished by a steam engine were used to propel and brake the cars. From the top, tracks were laid ten miles to the settlement of Moody, where an engine house, repair shops, and a warehouse were constructed. A hotel, saloon, general store, and post office were built during the boom, but a promised tan oak bark mill never materialized. Then disaster struck, bringing a temporary halt to the vulnerable transportation system that served the region. Two men were working on the Bear Harbor wharf on November 21, 1899, when a giant rogue wave rolled in from the west, lifted the dock, and tore it to pieces. As the wave receded, one man was seen clinging to a bush on the nearby bluff. He was rescued. The second man was never seen again.

A vast forest consisting of fifteen thousand acres of redwood, Douglas fir, and tan oak, along with the facilities at Bear Harbor, Moody, and what would become Andersonia, were purchased in 1903 by Henry Neff Anderson, who sought, like others, to put his mark upon the landscape. Huge trestles held in place by tall redwoods and long tunnels drilled through rock extended the railroad seven miles from Moody to Andersonia. A large dam, ten lumber camps, a mill, a town, and a house on a hill for Anderson were hewed out of the wilderness. The owner inspected the almost-completed mill in late 1905, but he never lived to see it operate. Anderson was struck on the head by a falling timber and died. Later, strong tremors from the San Francisco earthquake of 1906 did extensive damage to the fragile structures. The Bear Valley school closed two years later, signaling the end of that settlement. Moody and Andersonia melted back into the landscape.

Near the start of the five-mile trail that leads south from Bear Valley to Wheeler, the narrow track passes through a patch of redwoods named the J. Smeaton Chase Grove. Chase set out in 1910 to traverse the entire coastline on a horse. As happens periodically, California was on the cusp of change, with the Panama Canal about to be completed and automobiles already on the road. Chase wanted to see the state before its past disappeared. He rode south from Los Angeles to San Diego the first year, and then continued his journey from Los Angeles northward in May of 1911. By fall of that year he was in the Lost Coast country. He wrote, "We entered now a wonderful tract of forest, the finest I had seen, and evidently virgin, for there was no mark of either cutting or fire." The day was clear and hot, as autumn days on the North Coast can be. "It was an immense relief when evening shades came with delicious temperature, and I rode on leisurely through the grateful gloom, catching glimpses through forest windows of a gorgeous sunset that dulled and died imperceptibly into the clear indigo of nightfall."[3]

I hiked the trail on a similar day. From the redwood trees in the canyon of the Chase Grove, the trail ascended to the top of steep slopes that fall precipitously to the sparkling Pacific Ocean and the silent, white-fringed surf that defines offshore rocks. The trail eventually dropped through shaded School Marm Grove and the recently deserted logging settlement of Wheeler. School Marm Grove, now a campsite on the coastal trail, had been the site of a small red schoolhouse that also served as the community center. Approximately thirty students in grades one through six and one teacher were its weekday occupants. On weekends there were church services and Sunday school. Evenings there were potluck dinners, dances, and various social and community gatherings.

The air here had once been filled with the roar of logging trucks revving up to tackle the steep grade or downshifting on the descent from Usal Road, the screech of band saws, and smoke from the kiln. A freak windstorm tore the roofs off structures, scattered lumber, damaged water pipes to the extent that residents thought it was a heavy rainstorm, and silenced the diesel engines that furnished power to the logging camp. The inhabitants were amazed by the sudden quiet. The only remains of a bustling industrial complex that I could find were a few moss-encrusted concrete piers, partially covered by leaves, that had been a foundation for some type of structure, a small patch of asphalt roadway, and a rusted rectangular form that had supported a drum and cable system.

Wheeler had a brief, intense existence from 1950 to 1960. Its genealogy was extensive for its short life, indicating a frenzied hunt for riches. The Wolf Creek Timber Company, Warm Springs Lumber Company, Pacific Coast Company, Union Lumber Company, Boise Cascade Corporation, and the Georgia-Pacific Corporation were successive owners. When the last owner departed, all the structures were burned to the ground, leaving the smoke blowing through the vestigial forest.

Up the abandoned road from Wheeler, and near the headwaters of Little Jackass Creek, is the Sally Bell Grove, named for a Native American. No one knows who the first human inhabitants of the Lost Coast were; but the Sinkyone people, speaking a variation of the Athabascan language, arrived around 1400. The Shelter Cove Sinkyone, consisting of four tribelets in eighteen villages, occupied what would become the state wilderness area. They migrated with the seasons, moving from the warmer, sheltered inland valleys to the more exposed coast along narrow, steep pathways.

In the coastal waters there were salmon, steelhead, smelt, marine mammals, shellfish, and seaweed. On land there were beached whales, black-tailed deer, elk, and tan oak acorns whose meal was prized by the Indians for its delicious flavor. Fire was both a useful tool to cultivate the woodlands and meadows and an inadvertent danger.

The coast redwood served many purposes. The Sinkyone pursued seals and sea lions in canoes fashioned from downed redwood logs hollowed out with fire and obsidian-tipped tools. Their shelters were either conical or wedge-shaped and were fashioned from thick slabs of redwood bark bound to poles with iris fiber. The bark was peeled from the trees with elk-horn wedges and a stone maul. One of the materials woven into their baskets was redwood root fibers.

Up until the early 1850s, there were a little more than two thousand Sinkyone Indians occupying 350 square miles. "They were a people that got along with little," wrote University of California anthropologist A. L. Kroeber, "[and] that little the common stock of themselves and their neighbors, and as impartially the neighbors on one side as the other."[4] Fifty years later there were a hundred. The language was eventually lost, and the group never gained official status as a tribe.

One of the Sinkyone who survived into the 1930s was Sally Bell. Sally was a young girl when the acorn crop failed one year. The Sinkyone and other Indians pilfered livestock and potatoes from white settlers. The settlers in Mendocino County petitioned the local Indian agent, stating that they were about to "exterminate" the Indians unless a schooner-load of potatoes was delivered. No potatoes arrived, and what became known as the 1859–1860 "Mendocino Wars" were waged indiscriminately by a private army against all Indians. After holding hearings in the region, a special committee of the California Legislature condemned the whites and said more Indians had been killed during those two years than during the entire eighty years of Spanish and Mexican rule.

Sally lived with her family and other Sinkyones at Needle Rock. It was ten o'clock in the morning when the white men appeared.

They killed my grandfather and my mother and my father. I saw them do it. I was a big girl at the time. Then they killed my baby sister and cut her heart out and threw it in the brush where I ran and hid. My little sister was a baby, just crawling around. I didn't know what to do. I was so scared that I guess I just hid there a long time with my little sister's heart in my hands. I felt so bad and I was so scared that I just couldn't do anything else. Then I ran into the woods and hid there for a long time. I lived there a long time with a few other people who had got away. We lived on berries and roots and we didn't dare build a fire because the white men might come back after us. So we ate anything we could get. We didn't have clothes after a while, and we had to sleep under logs and in hollow trees because we didn't have anything to cover ourselves with, and it was cold then—in the spring. After a long time, maybe two, three months, I don't know how long, but sometime in the summer, my brother found me and took me to some white folks who kept me until I was grown and married.[5]

Sally later saved the life of a white baby. In 1901, when Roy Cathey was about to be born, the Garberville doctor didn't arrive on time at Four Corners on the ridge above Needle Rock, so Sally delivered the baby. "It was three o'clock in the morning, and I was a blue baby," Cathey recalled years later. "Well, she mumbled something to old Tom in Injun, and he took off. He come back, Dad said, with a bunch of roots about like that and she had a pot of water goin', she threw them roots in there and steeped it up, whatever it was. Dad said just quick as I took it, I commenced to perk up. Now what it was, I don't know." Cathey referred to Sally as "the old squaw with the hundred eleven on her chin."[6] Sinkyone women were tattooed with three vertical lines on their chins. Sally was the last full-blooded Sinkyone Indian.

In the early 1980s, Georgia-Pacific wanted to cut the redwoods in the Sally Bell Grove. People chained themselves to trees, there were arrests, and a lawsuit halted Georgia-Pacific's logging operations in the Sinkyone. A deal was cut, and seventy-one hundred acres were purchased by conservation-oriented groups. About half the acreage filled out the state wilderness area to its present boundaries. The remaining thirty-nine hundred acres on the east side of Usal Road—the drier, second-growth Douglas fir and tan oak forest—were held for "multiple-use" purposes, which could, and still might, include logging.

With a gift of $1.3 million from the Lannan Foundation, eleven federally recognized California Indian tribes took possession of the thirty-nine hundred acres extending north from Usal, under a conservation easement to be monitored by the Pacific Forest Trust, which specializes in saving private forests. The goal was to regrow a mature redwood, fir, and tan oak forest, encourage the revival of Indian forest customs and crafts, provide Native American employment and income from limited ecotourism, and extend the public trail system and establish camping sites.

I recently passed through the Indian lands. What was most conspicuous were the posted signs stating Wilderness Unlimited, No Trespassing, Avoid Arrest, Members Only, and Patrolled Area and the steel gates blocking access to dirt roads. The Usal campground, at the southern end of the state wilderness area, was badly degraded. Banned off-road vehicles had carved up the creek bed, ocean-side bluffs, and beach while state park officials in Sacramento were putting the final touches on a bravely worded master plan for this area.

Point Reyes is a bold, dark, rocky headland, nearly
600 feet high, and the western and higher extremity
of a ridge running east and west for 3 miles. There is a
low land northward of it, so that from northward and
southward it is usually made as an island, and also from
sea-ward in hazy weather. . . . Some farm produce, fish
and clams are shipped from here to San Francisco.
Communications may be had by rail and telegraph from
several points near the head of the bay. No directions
can be given that would be of value to a stranger.
United States Coast Pilot, 1909

THE AGRICULTURAL COAST

Point Reyes Station, named for nearby Point Reyes,
faces an abandoned railroad station. The town and
surrounding region have had one product—butter—
since the 1850s, when a 57,066-acre tract was acquired
by three men and leased to dairy farmers who began
to ship their butter to San Francisco by schooner.
The WPA Guide to California, **1939**

Agriculture reaches its most intensive development
along the central coast, but is in a state of decline here
as elsewhere on a shoreline that has become a hot real
estate property. Farmhouses and barns are plastered
with "for sale" signs or left to rot gracefully into the
ground. **Philip L. Fradkin,** *California,* **1974**

The Gulf of the Farallones National Marine Sanctuary
has been established to protect and preserve the marine
birds and mammals, their habitats, and other natural
resources in the waters surrounding the Farallon Islands
and Point Reyes, and to ensure the continued availability
of the area as a research and recreational resource.
United States Coast Pilot, 2006

t is a summer Saturday morning in Point Reyes Station, just north of San Francisco and at the head of Tomales Bay. Time for the weekly farmer's market—part marketplace, part social event, and part lesson in agricultural virtue and fervor. The spoken and written words *artisan, heirloom, organic, grass-fed, sustainable, natural, healthy, farm fresh,* and *local* are the lingua franca. In this small coastal town of fewer than one thousand inhabitants that serves as the commercial hub for a wider area in western Marin County, the word *locavore,* meaning someone who buys or eats food grown locally, was coined by a clerk in a bookstore who had a radio program on the local nonprofit FM station. West Marin is a place where such world leaders in the local food movement as Prince Charles, Alice Waters, Wendell Berry, and Michael Pollan visit and feel at home. It is also a place that serves as an example of a farm community, once the site of a dying, traditional, commodity-based agriculture, that reinvented itself as a thriving purveyor of recession-sensitive, high-end, niche products. In the process, innovative ways were found to preserve both open space and family farms.

To understand West Marin and the Point Reyes Peninsula in particular, the area's insular character needs to be understood. California got its name from a Spanish romance written in 1510 about a magical island whose inhabitants had weapons made of gold, and which was ruled by a black Amazon queen named Califia. The state is sealed off from the remainder of the nation by mountain ranges and a river. Marin County is a peninsula within the nation-state of California. The Point Reyes Peninsula is cut off from the mainland by the San Andreas Fault, the dividing line between the Pacific and North American tectonic plates. The ridges of the Coast Range are a physical and cultural divide between the east and west portions of the county. Although lacking weapons made of a precious metal, the inhabitants of Marin County are among the wealthiest in the nation.

No longer the site of a monoculture of cows producing cheese, butter, milk, and beef, as it was one hundred years ago when those products contained no adjectival modifiers beyond the designation of where they were grown, Point Reyes has in recent years blossomed with agricultural products bearing mouth-watering descriptions and healthy implications. They resemble the multiplicity of foods seasonally hunted and gathered within a radius of a few miles by the former Native American inhabitants. From a system of tenant farming, introduced by the first Anglo outsiders who came from New England, ranching within the boundaries of the Point Reyes National Seashore has reverted back to tenant-based agriculture. Being a tenant of the National Park Service within the Point Reyes National Seashore, however, has distinct economic advantages.

Outside the national seashore, restrictive county zoning ordinances that favored retaining agriculture, and the voluntary acceptance of the monetary inducements of a nonprofit land trust, have been incentives for succeeding generations of farm families to remain on the land. A multigenerational identification with a single place is highly unusual in California, where transience has been the dominant human characteristic. One fifth-generation farm family in West Marin traces the acquisition of its property back to the 1862 sale of six hundred acres by Henry W. Halleck, chief of staff of the Union Army during the Civil War. The preservation of small-scale agriculture in West Marin that serves as a model for other farm communities can best be understood within its historical context.

The Coast Miwok, whose presence in West Marin dates to A.D. 500 or thereabouts, were preceded by earlier and unknown Native American groupings extending back to 6000 B.C. The latter periodically occupied or transited the deep forests, rolling hills, fertile valleys, and exposed coastal and calmer bay waters. The abundance of food that could be harvested from the water or on land made possible a Native American population that, at the time of the first contact with Europeans, exceeded the depressed ranching-dominated population in the mid-twentieth century.

The English pirate Francis Drake, the first known outsider to visit this land, and his crew of eighty-seven on board the leaking *Golden Hinde,* loaded with treasure looted from the Spanish, landed in mid-June of 1579 at "a convenient and fit harborough." Most probably the site was the mouth of Drakes Estero, which empties into Drakes Bay, which, in turn, is contained within the sheltering arc of the Point Reyes Peninsula. They remained for five weeks, repairing the ship for its homeward journey and observing the many curious Miwoks, whom the English conveniently thought worshiped them as gods and had deeded them the land that Drake claimed as Nova Albion for his queen.

During the "nipping colds" of a typical foggy June and early July, the English noted the agricultural customs of the Indians, the first locavores. Inland from the cold, bare coast was "a goodly country, and fruitful soyle, stored with many blessings fit for the use of man." The strong, fleet Indians seldom missed catching a fish. "Very large and fat Deere," perhaps the native elk because of their size, and pocket gophers were sources of meat and skins. Acorns and roots were eaten raw, roasted, or ground up into fine meal and made into bread.[1]

Two Miwok words were recorded phonetically and handed down by transcribers of the voyage's log as *petah* and *tobah,* mistakenly thought to mean potato and tobacco, words unknown to the Miwoks but part of the vocabulary of the English. More likely *petah* was the potato-like squawroot or soaproot, and *tobah,* used in a ceremony, was Jimsonweed, a powerful narcotic. Both grew in the immediate area, as does illegally cultivated marijuana today. Checker mallow was steamed in an earth oven, and cow parsnip and showy Indian clover were eaten raw.

Other Native American culinary details were added after the establishment of the San Rafael Mission in 1817 and a written record. Mussels, clams, and oysters were gathered from Tomales Bay. (Oysters are commercially grown in the bay today and, as of this writing, in Drakes Estero, where there is a conflict with wilderness values.) At times the Native Americans denuded the landscape and drove species to near extinction. Grizzly and black bears disappeared with the coming of the Europeans and their riatas, lances, and rifles. There once were giant condors here. A few survive in central California. Smaller turkey buzzards now gracefully work the updrafts.

Converts came from the Tomales Bay region to be baptized at the new mission, and the Spanish priests traveled to West Marin to baptize the sick who could not make the trip. Some Miwoks found Spanish rule heavy-handed and fled north to the Russian colonies at Bodega Bay and Fort Ross, where they were paid for their work, and where they intermarried with Russians and other native peoples.

The Russians called their colony Nova Albion after Drake's appellation, and searched for sea otters and silver mines. They were most successful at raising livestock and fruit, but could not feed their countrymen in Alaska, which was the prime reason for their moving southward to the one stretch of the California coast not under Spanish or Mexican control. Their stay lasted only thirty years, and they departed in 1841.

Longhorn cattle from the San Rafael Mission drifted westward to the coast. These first four-legged invaders, to be followed by many thousands more, were prized not for their milk or meat but for their remains. Their hides and tallow were transported to San Francisco Bay and to such vessels as the brig *Pilgrim*, on which the Harvard-educated Richard Henry Dana served as a sailor. The crew of that brig spent most of December 1835 loading such cargo. In his book *Two Years Before the Mast*, Dana predicted: "If California ever becomes a prosperous country, this bay will be at the centre of its prosperity."[2] Dating from this time, agricultural products from West Marin would be transported by ship, then train and truck, to San Francisco.

The regime changes were dizzying, the first Native Americans having been followed by the Miwoks, English, Spanish, Russians, Mexicans, and Americans. Naval Lieutenant Joseph Warren Revere, a native of Massachusetts and grandson of Paul Revere, traveled to Punta de los Reyes in 1846 on an inspection trip after raising the American flag in Sonoma and becoming the commandant of the Northern District of California. Revere stopped in August at the Olema rancho of Rafael Garcia, a former corporal at the San Rafael Mission who had received one of the first land grants in the area. The lieutenant set out on an elk hunt with Garcia's neighbors. They spotted a herd of "not less than four hundred head of superbly fat animals" and gave chase on their horses. Revere shot a doe and her fawn. Six fat elks were killed by various means, and the remainder of the herd was either wounded or scattered. The party gorged on the delicacies, reduced the remaining fatty parts to tallow, and used the hides to transport the tallow back to the rancho. Revere wrote of Point Reyes and its agricultural possibilities:

The Punta Reyes is a favorite hunting-ground, the elk being attracted by the superior quality of the pasture—the land lying so near the sea, that the dews are heavy and constant, adding great luxuriance to the wild oats and other grains and grasses. The elk are very abundant at this season, and more easily killed than cattle. We passed many places, on our way back, where moldering horns and bones attested to the wholesale slaughter which had been made in previous years by the rancheros of the neighborhood.[3]

Joseph Revere adopted the first name of José and remained in the county, purchasing a rancho in San Geronimo Valley that he claimed ran to the coast. He and his friend Garcia took part in another chase, this

1. *(Previous page)* Driftwood in surf. Mattole Beach, Lost Coast, 2007. 2. *(Right)* Oceanscape, looking south from the Marin Headlands, 2010.

3. Beach named Gaviota, meaning "seagull," after a seagull was killed there by early Spanish explorers. Gaviota State Park, 2006.

4. *(Left)* Fog, and a power plant's three stacks. Morro Bay, 2007.

5. *(Below)* Morro Bay Rock at dawn. Morro Bay, 2007.

6. The Franciscan Formation punctured by Tobin's Tunnel, where the San Andreas Fault temporarily heads out to sea. Daly City, 2009.

7. Emergency-vehicle tracks in sand, left after a man was buried alive under a collapsing bluff. Ocean Beach, San Francisco, 2006.

8. Eli under the Great Highway. Ocean Beach, San Francisco, 2006.

9. Tatiana behind glass. Laguna Beach, 2007.

10. Home perched on rocks. Carmel, 2010.

11. *(Previous spread)* Looking south toward the U.S.-Mexico border. Border Field State Park, 2006.

12. *(Right)* New and "improved" fence. U.S.-Mexico border, Border Field State Park, 2010.

13. First tattoo. Venice Beach, 2007.

14. Tom and his guitar in racquetball court. Venice Beach, 2006.

15. *(Left)* Oil rigs, stars, moon, and passing aircraft. Huntington Beach, 2009.

16. *(Below)* Site of massive 1969 oil spill. Santa Barbara Channel, 2006.

17. Mavericks Surf Contest, a giant-wave competition. Pillar Point, Half Moon Bay, 2010.

18. Harbor seals, tourists, onlookers, and this photographer. La Jolla, 2010.

19. Dead bird picked clean. Rodeo Beach, Sausalito, 2008.

20. Discarded jacket along U.S.-Mexico border. Border Field State Park, 2010.

21. Woman walking her dogs. Seal Beach, 2006.

22. Bridge workers descending stairs in fog. Golden Gate Bridge, San Francisco, 2006.

23. Tijuana Estuary, one of the most polluted waterways in the United States. U.S.-Mexico border, Border Field State Park, 2010.

24. *(Right)* Cow paths on farmland, and road to lighthouse. Point Reyes, 2005.

25. *(Following page)* Homes on the edge, ruins of a roadway, and an old railroad grade in the background. Daly City, 2005.

one involving Indians, who were regarded as chattel by their pursuers. The two men needed cheap farm laborers, so they raided Indian villages that lay two days' ride to the north, taking their Indian vaqueros with them to trap "their wild relatives." Weapons were employed, but there was no mention of casualties or deaths in Revere's account. The laborers were acquired, said Revere, in the manner of the times and taken to his rancho to manufacture adobe bricks. They were paid with shirts and blankets.[4] Rafael Garcia and José Revere were defendants in a land-title-and-boundary legal action filed by the Shafter brothers, New England lawyers who would soon take over the entire Point Reyes Peninsula and institute the first tenant-farming system, ushering in the American ranching era.

In a broad sense, the story of agriculture on the Point Reyes Peninsula from 1836 to 1939 is reflected in the fates of the Garcia and Shafter families. What their stories illustrate is the transitory nature of the proprietorship of land, whether by individuals or tribes or the nations who laid claim to West Marin. The first date in this two-family saga, 1836, is when Garcia acquired his land grant. The last, 1939, is when the last Shafter properties were sold.

The manner in which Native Americans were acquired as slaves for the Mexican ranch owners had been established before Revere's arrival. In the summer of 1845, Garcia and a fellow rancher led a raiding party on Indian villages in Sonoma County. They beat, killed, and captured their quarry on their way to Fort Ross, which had been sold to John Sutter of Sacramento by the Russians four years earlier. Seven of the raiders, including Garcia, gang-raped two Indian women in the home of the fort's absent white caretaker. They would not let one of their Indian vaqueros participate in the rapes because he was not a *gente de razon*, as persons of Spanish descent referred to themselves. The home and the adjacent Indian village were pillaged.

When they went to split up the spoils, there were fistfights among the raiders. A Contra Costa rancher who had a record of purchasing Indian children as slaves took 150 of the prisoners. Garcia acquired a dozen families. Because the acts of violence had been so overt, there was a trial. (There is no record of a judgment.) A few months later at the San Rafael Mission, Garcia became godfather to six young Indians, most probably acquired in the raid. Betty Goerke wrote in her book about the Miwok of Marin County: "In the North Bay, according to most accounts by the settlers and the military, the Indians were pursued for capture rather than murder, because the rancho owners needed men to work as laborers. The goal may have been different, but the outcome was the same: murder, rape, and enslavement."[5]

Garcia prospered, but his time to experience the fate of minorities would come. The land-, slave-, horse-, hog-, sheep-, and cattle-rich former corporal moved from Bolinas to Olema near the head of Tomales Bay. He settled into a sumptuous adobe rancho on disputed ground that would become the site for the structures of the next two land barons—the showplace ranch of the Shafter dairy enterprise and the present-day headquarters of Point Reyes National Seashore. Sheltered from the battering coastal winds and within the gentle folds of the wooded

Inverness and Bolinas ridges that enclosed Olema Valley, Garcia lived the life of a patriarch. His celebrations were legendary, and his visitors and family were numerous.

The rules changed again when California became a state in 1850. The following year the tax assessor in the newly created county of Marin valued Garcia's property far above any of his coastal neighbors'. Beginning in 1852 and continuing for a dozen years, Garcia and others were enmeshed in a tangle of lawsuits over land claims that drained his cash resources. Garcia died in 1866, four months after finally gaining legal title to three thousand acres of what had once been a ninety-five-hundred-acre ranch. His widow was killed by a thwarted suitor, and by 1880 most of the remaining Garcia lands were in the hands of the Shafters and other recent settlers.

Oscar and James Shafter came from a prominent New England family. Oscar arrived in California in 1854 after losing a bid for the governorship of Vermont. After serving in the Vermont and Wisconsin legislatures, James joined his brother the following year. They practiced law together, quickly rose to political and legal prominence, and in 1857, by acquiring land in Point Reyes in lieu of legal fees, began to build their holdings in West Marin into what would become "the first large-scale and high-quality dairies in the state." At one time the Shafters' butter operation was touted as being the largest in the world.[6]

Marin County led the state in the quality of its butter and volume of dairy products well into the 1890s, with the Shafters' holdings making up the bulk of production. "There is probably no better dairy country in the world than Sonoma and Marin coun-

ties," crowed a history of the latter county, where the cows graze "in clovers and native grasses up to their eyes, and are fat and sleek, and almost uncomfortable with their well-filled milk bags."[7]

Oscar's son-in-law Charles Webb Howard joined the two Shafters as a partner. After gobbling up the Garcia and other properties, the three men controlled the entire peninsula, excluding the northern tip and the southern area around Bolinas. They divided the peninsula into three shares, and then subdivided them further into smaller farm units with alphabetical designations from A to Z, and names matching distinctive natural features at the southern end, where they ran out of letters. The partners were very careful in their selection of tenant farmers, choosing only those who were "men of capital,—sober, industrious, enterprising, and [who] have their families with them." Their contract terms were "good and encouraging," said Oscar, who deemed that "the best policy in the long run."[8] In county, state, and national publications, the thirty-one dairy ranches were praised for their productivity, their cleanliness, and the quality of their products.

There was an unwritten caste system based on the ethnicity and skin color of the laborers and tenant farmers. Among the laborers were Chinese, Native Americans, and Portuguese from the Azores, the latter being singled out for criticism by native-born whites for coming to California, working for low wages, taking jobs from locals, and then buying productive land. While some Portuguese would join Irish, Italian-speaking Swiss, and a smattering of Scandinavian and other European immigrants in becoming the landed gentry, that was not an option for the Chinese, Japanese, and Native Americans, nor for the Latinos who arrived in the latter third of the twentieth century to work as farm laborers on land that had once been owned by other Spanish speakers. By the late twentieth century, the cost of land had skyrocketed, and the only people who could afford large parcels had either owned them for years or were wealthy outsiders. West Marin would remain an Anglo-European enclave—an island in time in both physical and racial aspects—while the remainder of the state became multiracial.

Butter imprinted with the initials P. R. enclosed within a diamond shape, indicating quality, and cheeses, rather than milk, which spoiled rapidly, were shipped to San Francisco in shallow-draft schooners from wharves in Bolinas and the sheltered bays on both sides of the peninsula. A railroad financed by a syndicate headed by James Shafter arrived in Point Reyes Station at the head of Tomales Bay in 1875. The trains delivered dairy products to Sausalito, from where they were ferried across the bay. Gradually more milk was shipped, particularly after 1922, when a good road from West Marin made faster delivery by trucks possible.

Shortly after the start of the twentieth century, J. Smeaton Chase, traveling northward on his plodding coastal journey, passed through this region in September, normally the time of year when the warm, fogless days of a real summer follow the windy, fog-filled days of the preceding months. It is also a time of stasis, of waiting, hoping, and in some cases praying for change in the form of fall rains that transform the brown, trampled grasses to vivid green shoots by Christmas.

The outer coastal road passed through Bolinas and the southernmost Shafter properties. Chase found it "a quiet, treeless land with an occasional dairy-farm staring from the brown hillsides." He sought food and shelter for himself and his horse. The heavily grazed pastures, he noted, "had been exhausted to a point" that meant starvation for a working horse. Chase stopped at one farm, but no one was home. It was getting late. An Italian-Swiss brother and sister, who could barely speak English, gave Chase and his horse shelter and food. He proceeded on his way the next morning after a hog had rifled his saddlebag during the night and relieved him of a loaf of bread, two pounds of bacon, half an unused notebook, and some revolver cartridges.[9]

Chase rode through Lake Ranch at the southern end of what would become the Point Reyes National Seashore.

The country here was very interesting in appearance. A group of small fresh-water lakes lies near the shore, which rises to a picturesque moorland backed by irregular hills. Seaward, the Farallones showed like icebergs on the sky-line, and the long arm of Point Reyes marked the outline of Drake's Bay. Hours passed without a sign of human life: once or twice a deer appeared in some glade among the brush, and frequent coveys of quail whirred away as we put them up. This is a magnificent game country, and the fact has not been overlooked by the sporting clubs, whose notices hailed me on all sides with threats of Severe Penalties and Utmost Rigors.[10]

The coastal traveler continued to the edge of Drakes Estero and noted the white cliffs that had reminded Drake of the white cliffs of Dover and, thus, had led to the name Nova Albion. The wind was "rattling" from the northwest, and he saw nothing special about the place except "the old simplicity of cliff and sea," which he had encountered elsewhere on his journey.[11] That night was spent in an Olema hotel. The next day Chase passed along the north shore of Tomales Bay, where he noted a settlement, near oyster beds, picturesquely named Bivalve and the "modestly" named settlement of Hamlet. To the Southern Californian the "repulsive" wind was cold, biting, and unceasing, and "neither of us was in a very cheerful humor."[12] Horse and rider pressed on to more sheltered Tomales, where they "exchanged the vague discomforts of the road for the concrete misery of a typical country hotel."[13]

The Shafters, whose land Chase had traversed, believed that Point Reyes belonged to them because they were, in order of importance, New Englanders and Americans. Neither designation was enough to permit them to hold on to the land forever. "The Shafters and Howards," wrote a local historian, "had shown as little aptitude for land management as for personal happiness."[14] Personal reasons and economic necessities, brought on by the failure of the railroad and by the Depression, forced them to sell. They began to liquidate their holdings in 1919, speeded up the process during the Depression, and concluded it in 1939.

During the decline of the Shafters, former tenants, ranchers from elsewhere, and speculators purchased their holdings. Some held on to their properties briefly in order to make a quick profit. Others remained for longer periods of time. A few made it to the fifth generation and the present—the longevity of some ranching families being a distinguishing characteristic of the area. Gallagher, Mc-Clure, Kehoe, Lunny (Irish surnames); Grossi, Spaletta, Lucchesi (Swiss-Italian); and Nunes and Mendoza (Portuguese) are some of the longer-lasting names still attached to ranches in the area.

One rancher, Joe Mendoza, described how he got his start milking cows in the 1930s. As a teenager, he was responsible for milking about a dozen cows when he came home from grammar school. He first strapped a one-legged stool to his bottom. Sanitation was minimal. He wiped off the teats of the cow with a rag. As Mendoza milked, he hoped the cow would not kick over the pail. For years he dreamed that he hadn't removed the stool and was walking down main street with it still attached. He termed that dream the "dairyman's nightmare."

With freedom from the constraints of contracts that had tied them to cows, the ranchers attempted to farm a variety of crops, rather than just feed for livestock. The problem was that there was very little sheltered, watered, flat ground with good soil for raising vegetables and fruits. They made scattered attempts to raise row crops, growing beets, beans, and artichokes in the valleys. But the cost of farm laborers and the fact that such crops could be grown and brought to market more cheaply elsewhere meant the failure of truck farming. An attempt in the early 1930s to raise peas on a fairly large scale failed. "Nothing went according to plan," wrote the local historian. "The railroad pulled out, even before the first crop matured. The crop itself looked to be a beauty, only to wither within days—a 90 per cent loss."[15] A monoculture of dairy and beef cattle soon prevailed again.

The military, facing the perceived threat of an invasion by Japanese forces, took over large portions of the peninsula during World War II. Not all the restrictions enacted in the name of national security made sense. Ranchers of German and Italian descent were banished from the immediate shoreline, and Japanese farm laborers were imprisoned further inland. Bill Straus was a German Jew who had emigrated from Palestine in 1934 and had graduated from the University of California a few years later. He was considered an enemy alien. The dairy rancher, who lived on the inland side, was not allowed to cross Highway 1 in Marshall. His groceries and mail were delivered by a helpful storeowner on the landward side of the white line dividing the coastal highway. On the other side was Tomales Bay and all kinds of possible contacts with the enemy.

In the postwar years, the suburbanization of Los Angeles County drove dairies into the Central Valley, where the good roads enabled the large feedlot dairies to supply cheaper milk products to the San Francisco Bay Area. Beef cattle and sheep began replacing milk cows in West Marin, dairy ranches were sold or merged with other ranches, commercial establishments in the surrounding villages closed their doors, and it looked like a way of life would disappear as speculators and developers made plans to turn the coastal lands into lots for vacationers and tourist facilities. A nonfarm population of 125,000 that coincided with the overblown expectations of the impact of the establishment of a national seashore was envisioned in the 1960s.

The most recent years of farm history are bookended by the raising and lowering of the levees around 550 acres at the head of Tomales Bay. The construction in 1946 of those mounds of dirt armored with rock and studded with wooden floodgates set in concrete frames, and their subsequent dismantling in 2008, echoed the changes in national priorities over a span of six decades. To Waldo Giacomini, the rancher who owned the property, and the federal agencies that aided its conversion in 1946, marshland was wasteland. It needed to be put to productive use, meaning put to use generating income, not wildlife. Thirty years later, conservation no longer meant the reclamation of wetlands and their conversion to farmlands; it meant the restoration of marshlands to some type of historic natural condition. It took another thirty years to make that a reality in West Marin. The Giacomini family got caught in the middle of the switch in priorities. "The family's continued operation of the ranch has simply bumped innocently into a new set of values and awarenesses," said a fellow rancher.[16] The restored marsh was folded into the national seashore, and the two stories became one.

The movement to establish a national seashore that would eventually dislodge the dairy rancher and his family from the irrigated pastureland at the head of Tomales Bay had already commenced as the dikes, with federal funding, were being raised and a seasonal dam, with federal approval, was being constructed in the adjacent creek. The dam provided a swimming hole for the community, but it also blocked the salmon run.

The Park Service identified, in 1935, the potential of the peninsula for designation as a national park, and two small bites were taken out of existing ranches in 1938 and 1942 to create county parks on ocean beaches. A state park on Tomales Bay had its beginnings in 1945. Starting with tracts of redwoods, which included some coastal holdings, later focusing on coastal beaches and then the San Francisco Bay, volunteers mounted several successful crusades to "save" something. The conservationists were on a roll, and their movement soon extended to the Point Reyes Peninsula, a slumbering wilderness near a population of millions.

The ranchers didn't like what was happening. At best, it meant a return to the tenancy of the Shafter years; at worst, the outright acquisition of their land. The widow of one of the Shafter tenants asked at a congressional hearing in 1961: "What kind of recreation did I have when I was a youngster? I worked and saved so my children would have a sense of security and heritage that I felt belonged to them. Now every inch of my land is supposed to disappear."[17]

The widow, who stood in the way of a steamroller, didn't have a chance, although she and others would not suffer unduly. The conservation-minded Kennedy administration was in office, and a new national seashore had been established in President Kennedy's backyard on Cape Cod. Its equivalent on the West Coast was authorized in 1962. Ranchlands making up nearly one-third of the seventy-one-thousand-acre Point Reyes National Seashore were purchased and then leased back at favorable rates. Along with price supports for milk, it was another form of subsidy, but one that protected the rural quality and open space of the peninsula. The result was thirty-two thousand acres of officially declared wilderness, a sizeable herd

of reintroduced tule elk, and access and recreation for millions that was judged a public benefit.

Various devices were invented on the state, county, and local levels to prevent the carving up of farmlands for subdivisions outside the new national seashore. What transpired in California, and particularly in Marin County, would have been considered a communist plot or an unconstitutional taking of land elsewhere in the West, where there is a fierce sense of individualism and property rights. The state legislature passed the Williamson Act in the mid-1960s, which provided for reduced tax assessments on farmland that continued to be used as such, and the owners of the 650-acre Green Gulch Farm on the southern Marin coast were the first to sign up for that program. Nearly sixteen million acres of farmland throughout the state are now protected by that act. By a three-to-two vote, the county supervisors zoned all agricultural lands a minimum sixty acres in the 1970s, and development slowed to a trickle. Fearing the supervisors' action was not permanent and could be reversed, a coalition of ranchers and environmentalists founded the Marin Agricultural Land Trust in 1980. Now a national model, the land trust has acquired agricultural conservation easements that permanently protect more than forty thousand acres on more than sixty family farms.

All these measures, and the morphing of the rancher-environmental coalition into a group that is exploring how to manage and protect diverse interests on a watershed basis, could not have occurred if the region did not have a unique blend of highly unusual characteristics. Marin lies a soaring bridge length from San Francisco to the south and is a bastion of liberal politics. It is home to San Quentin Prison, George Lucas's Skywalker Ranch, a Frank Lloyd Wright–designed civic center, and, as of this writing, houses owned by both of California's United States senators. There is also great wealth in the form of the nonprofit Marin Community Foundation, one of the largest community foundations in the country. At the level of local government—where it counts the most in terms of land use—county supervisors since the mid-1970s have bridged the divide between West and East Marin and have acted in concert with the rancher-environmental coalition.

With a culture of agricultural unity in place, a new type of farming began to emerge. As with butter in the nineteenth century, finer farm products were aimed at smaller markets. It began in Bolinas as a communal venture by hippies and highly educated urban dropouts during the back-to-the-land movement of the early 1970s, a time when traditional agriculture was in decline. An agricultural movement designed to grow smaller, organic crops and bring fresher produce to market spread during the ensuing decades. Field and row crops returned. Apples, artichokes, beans, berries, broccoli, cabbage, carrots, chard, cucumbers, eggs, garlic, herbs, leaf lettuce, mixed salad greens, onions, parsley, potatoes, spinach, squash, tomatoes, turnips, and watercress now bear an organic label issued in Marin County.

Younger generations from traditional West Marin farm families went off to such agricultural institutions of higher learning as Cal Poly at San Luis Obispo, Fresno State University, and the University of California at Davis and returned (a miracle in itself not experienced in many other farm communities) with the marketing skills, business acumen, and cultural values that appealed to the new customer base. Between the affluent and the educated, suburbanites and ranchers, and the two Marins there developed "a bonding and synergy," in the words of a University of California agricultural official, "that hasn't occurred elsewhere."[18] Such local brand names with national reputations as the Straus Family and Cowgirl creameries, Niman Ranch and Marin Sun Farm meats, Hog Island Oyster Company, Point Reyes Farmstead Cheese Company, and Star Route Farms sell their farm products to fine restaurants, gourmet food stores, supermarkets, and other food outlets across the country.

More than two million tourists swell the local population during a year. Referring to the lighthouse on the point, a 2008 headline over a story in the *San Francisco Chronicle* trumpeted: "Where Foodies Can See the Light: Point Reyes has become a West Marin beacon—not just for its beauty, but for its bounty." This is a small community, which unfortunately is getting crowded on weekends, that being the price of agricultural success.

Next day was the equinox, and the morning was dull, threatening (or, a better way of putting it, promising) rain. We were early on the road, which rounded the head of [Half Moon Bay], passing through a number of new-born "cities" whose existence was to be known mainly by pitiful little cement sidewalks, already bulging and broken. Each place in succession adjured me by stentorian sign-boards not to miss the wealth that awaited investors in its "gilt-edged" lots. It was a boon to exchange the songs of these financial sirens for the charms of a sea and sky alike of wistful gray, lighted ever and anon by gleams of gold that bore no hint of real estate. **J. Smeaton Chase, 1911**

THE RESIDENTIAL COAST

As soon as we ascended to the summit we descried a great bay formed by a point of land which runs far out into the open sea and looks like an island. Farther out, about west-northwest from where we stood and a little to the southwest of the point, six or seven white far-allones of different sizes were to be seen. Following the coast of the bay to the north some white cliffs are visible, and to the northwest is the mouth of an estuary which seems to penetrate into the land. In view of these signs, and of what is stated in the itinerary of the pilot Cabrera Bueno, we came to the recognition of this port; it is that of Our Father San Francisco, and we have left that of Monterey behind. **Fray Juan Crespí, diarist of the Portolá expedition, upon sighting San Francisco Bay from a ridge just south of Pacifica in 1769**

Here, within the space of a few miles, is the counterpart of the dense tract developments in southern California that northerners like to mock. **Philip L. Fradkin, *California*, 1974**

From Point Montara for 2.5 miles to Point San Pedro the coast is bold and rugged, rising sharply from the sea to the spurs extending from Montara Mountain. Devils Slide is light-colored and is the highest bluff in this locality. The highway cuts are distinctive features in the bluffs. ***United States Coast Pilot*, 2006**

When the waves build in intensity, when the storm that has traversed the wide Pacific Ocean finally arrives, when torrential rains descend, and when the land starts slipping and sliding at speeds of up to forty miles per hour, then solid chunks of earth, trees, rocks and boulders, asphalt and concrete, fences, parts of homes and their furnishings, and sometimes human bodies tumble down steep slopes, through canyons, over cliffs, and into the ocean, where the currents, waves, and tides disperse the frothy, light-brown stew. When the waves decrease and all seems safe and serene again, people begin to build—or rebuild, as the case may be—fortresslike revetments to protect their homes from the next disaster.

The process of erecting barriers and anchoring sliding land is called armoring, a military term. It involves concrete, shotcrete, gunite, wooden beams and planks, soil nails, steel mesh and steel anchors, rocks and boulders, broken asphalt and concrete, car bodies, steel beams, sheets of heavy plastic, and interlocking concrete *dolosse,* which resemble children's jacks and weigh up to forty tons. Two of the most common types of buffers are seawalls and bulkheads, the two terms being interchangeable, and riprap, meaning engineered rock barriers.

From Crescent City to Imperial Beach, one hundred and ten miles, or 10 percent, of the coast is armored, mostly in the southernmost counties. "There is no such thing as permanent protection," state the knowledgeable authors of *Living with the Changing California Coast.*[1] The sea level rises, one property's protection focuses wave energy on another, materials

disintegrate or are undercut by wave action, and the waves continue to pound relentlessly, the currents to sweep, and the sand on which California's beach mythology is based drifts away.

Daly City, Pacifica, and Half Moon Bay in San Mateo County provide vivid examples of the destructive nature of coastal landslides. The effects of fire are more prevalent to the south. Like nearly every other section of the coastline—and the state for that matter—San Mateo County has a history of serial disasters. Here, at one time, there was a tunnel for carriages and a railroad built precariously along the face of a fragile cliff, and when both failed, these initial attempts at providing transportation corridors to convey residents were doomed by construction of a state highway built on top of the abandoned railroad right-of-way. Yet another tunnel and highway were under construction when I last visited the area.

The north-to-south journey along coastal San Mateo County begins at the northwest corner of Daly City, where there are houses and a small park teetering on the edges of cliffs straddling a yawning chasm that is an old landslide at the end of John Daly Boulevard. The five-hundred-foot cliffs, which rise to seven hundred feet further south, are composed of loose sandstones fractured by the nearby San Andreas Fault and its numerous offshoots and then saturated during the winter months by rainfall. This volatile mixture stands poised to slide during the next intensive rainstorm or earthquake.

The first coastal transportation route was a modest beach and cliff-side path traversed by Native Americans and then Spanish, Mexican, and American ranchers who drove cattle along the shoreline. San Francisco banker Richard M. Tobin wanted a more civilized route from his summer residence in what is now Pacifica, meaning a roadway that would accommodate a carriage. There was one obstacle, the tough outcrop of the Franciscan formation known as Mussel Rock. No problem, said Tobin and a few friends, who subscribed five thousand dollars to the first effort to defeat the intransigent ocean. It would be man over nature. The county newspaper applauded Tobin's efforts in 1874: "Since the birth of San Mateo County we have heard, times without number, of the utter impossibility of constructing a wagon road or railroad along the ocean coast." The solution was four separate tunnels, with a total length of 400 feet, blasted through the rock to a width and height of ten feet. The pounding surf and loose soil defeated that early effort a short time after the tunnels were completed. The fifty-foot portion of one tunnel that remains, it was reported in 1986, "serves today as merely a curiosity for the casual visitor," who, to see it, has to scramble down an abandoned landfill that emits methane gas.[2] The northernmost tunnel, built more than a century ago, has retained its shape in the hard rock, with chisel marks still intact. The access path to it on both sides has been demolished by the waves.

Construction of the Ocean Shore Railroad, planned to terminate in Santa Cruz but never reaching that destination, began in 1905. The granting of the franchise became temporarily mired at its San Francisco end in the municipal graft scandals of that time. The idea behind the railroad was not to provide transpor-

tation in its purest form so much as the means to sell land by transporting people to vacant ocean-side lots. Prospective communities along the way were given names that implied the vaguely familiar, exotic, and pleasurable: Long Island's Rockaway Beach, England's Brighton Beach, and Spain's Granada. Excursion trains bore such wistful names as the Mermaid Special. The considerable damage caused by the 1906 earthquake along the partially completed railroad right-of-way should have proved the futility of the venture, but it did not.

On top of what was called "the great earth-slump at Mussel Rock," which marks the incision of the San Andreas Fault, and for a distance of three miles to the north along the side of precipitous cliffs, the newly laid railroad tracks were periodically obliterated by landslides. Repairs were quickly made and construction continued. Rather than tunneling through the bluff above Mussel Rock, as had been done previously, the railroad company simply blasted its way across it. Greek immigrant construction crews drove a four-hundred-foot tunnel through the flanks of San Pedro Mountain at Point San Pedro, to the south, but repeated failures of the slope at Devil's Slide halted train traffic. The ill-conceived railroad with the slogan "Reaches the Beaches" was a financial disaster, and operations ceased in 1921. Shortly thereafter, bootleggers made use of the abandoned Tobin and Point San Pedro tunnels for storage of their contraband liquor.

In the late 1930s, when travel by automobiles became popular, work began along the old right-of-way on a scenic coastal highway. A route more scenic (provided the fog lifts) and more landslide prone could not have been chosen. Named variously State Route 1, the Coast Highway, and the Cabrillo Highway, the stretch from Thornton State Beach at the end of John Daly Boulevard to just past Mussel Rock functioned intermittently for twenty years. It was frequently closed due to landslides, erosion of the roadbed, heavy fogs, and strong winds. The stretch of roadway and its continuation south of Pacifica and past Devil's Slide proved dangerous to motorists and expensive to maintain for the state highway department, now known as Caltrans. The Daly City section was abandoned by Caltrans after the moderate 1957 earthquake, whose epicenter was located at Mussel Rock. Daly City attempted to maintain the cracked roadway for one year after the state abandoned it, and then the city also gave up. The coast highway was rerouted along the flat ridgetop to the east before dropping down to Pacifica and continuing through the problem-plagued Devil's Slide area.

The residential land developments that were being hastily slapped upon the windswept sand dunes south of San Francisco in the 1950s and 1960s were served by this vulnerable highway. None were more ambitious or widespread than the developments constructed by Henry Doelger. Between 1934 and 1941, Doelger mass-produced twenty thousand single-family homes in San Francisco's Sunset District. He repeated this successful formula to the south, in San Mateo County, adding apartments and shopping centers to the mix and earning Malvina Reynolds's wry lyrics: "Little boxes on the hillside / Little boxes made of ticky tacky / Little boxes on the hillside / Little boxes all the same."

Instead of singling out hillsides, Reynolds could

just as well have written about little boxes on the sides of eroding cliffs. Doelger homes need to be appreciated for what the seven basic designs represented, and that was relatively affordable single-family housing. What they are not, however, is safe structures in earthquake and flood country, mostly because some are poised on the edges of cliffs and all have a weak understory. The second floors are built over a garage set on unreinforced concrete pads that float on sand.

A recreational facility was created to serve the burgeoning population south of San Francisco. Thornton State Beach Park was established in 1963. A typewritten history of the park states, "Thornton Beach itself is a result of a large slump block or rotational landslide."[3] The parking lot was reached by a short access road off the abandoned coastal highway at the end of John Daly Boulevard. All three entities that would be deserted in their separate times—railroad, highway, and park—converged here. There was an office and restrooms at the park, and the small, graded parking lot was sealed with asphalt, and then resealed four years later to smooth over widening cracks. A landing strip was bulldozed in the 36,356-acre park for gliders, and the first glider landed in 1969. The glider project was then "shelved," according to the history. This section of the coast eventually became a popular hang-gliding spot. The office was used as a headquarters for volunteers who flocked to the beach to clean up a 1971 oil spill. The state beach was abandoned in the early 1980s after a series of fierce storms.

The modern era of destruction along the California coast began in late 1981 with a series of El Niño storms that continued for the next twenty years. It rained in the fall of 1981, and then it rained again and again until the soil was saturated to the point where it could not contain any more liquid without bursting. Over a period of thirty-four hours, extending from January 3 to January 5 in 1982, it rained in amounts up to twenty-five inches along a 160-mile stretch of the coastline from Sonoma County to Monterey County.

The land melted under the deluge. Thousands of landslides and debris flows, the latter a more viscous form of the former, burst from hillsides and carried everything in their paths to the ocean. Thirty-three people were killed and sixty-five hundred homes and numerous businesses, roads, bridges, electrical and sewer lines, and the state park in Daly City were either damaged or destroyed. In Pacifica to the south, there were exceptionally large amounts of rain, and 475 landslides killed three children, destroyed four homes, and caused millions of dollars' worth of damage. At a conference that convened a few months later at Stanford University, assembled experts agreed there had been "a general unawareness" that a storm of such magnitude would occur, and that there had been no adequate preparations. An expanding population and lax local controls over land use were blamed for making the Bay Area susceptible to such disasters.

There is a small overlook maintained by Daly City with interpretive signs that mention in a general manner the massive landslide and the nearby presence of the San Andreas Fault. There is no specific mention of the lost homes and roads and park or the continuing threat to what remains along the edge of this coast. The city council of Daly City refused an

effort endorsed by the U.S. Geological Survey to erect a sign in 2006 stating that the epicenter of the 1906 earthquake was just offshore. The city did not seek this type of notoriety.

Across the chasm from the overlook, the land continues to erode, taking with it streets and homes. Few are aware of the short but disastrous history of Lynvale Court and the area at the southern end of the Thornton Beach landslide, certainly not the potential buyers of 50 Roslyn Court. That Doelger-constructed house lies on the edge of the bluff at the northwest end of the street that is adjacent and runs parallel to the remains of Lynvale Court. A Daly City engineering and geologic report states, "Approximately 100 feet of landslide headscarp recession over the past 30 years has forced removal of 5 homes, and resulted in loss of approximately 80 feet of the western end of Lynvale Court. It threatens to undermine home sites on Lynvale Court and the northwest side of Roslyn Court."[4]

Grading for the homes on Lynvale and Roslyn Courts began in 1954. The failure of a thirty-inch storm drain buried in the bluff the following year caused a massive slide. Doelger's workers secured the eroded hillside with a concrete wall held in place by steel cables attached to steel deadmen sunk in the suspect terrain. There was little damage in the 1957 earthquake, but the storm drain system failed again during the winter of 1963, carrying away the face of the bluff below the abandoned roadbed that lay beneath the homes. A fissure appeared in the cul-de-sac at the end of Lynvale Court. Doelger and the state highway department argued over who was to blame.

The storm drain system failed for the third time

during the massive storms of 1981–1982, and the earth slipped, as it did throughout the region. Lynvale Court was shortened by fifty feet, and four houses were removed. A severe storm in February of 2004 caused the fourth failure of the storm drain system, and a wall of water cascaded over the lip of the bluff. Lynvale Court shrank again, to its present status as a stub street. One house was removed from the western side of Skyline Drive, which caps the two shorter courts and provides access to the escape route. Skyline Drive was also undermined, threatening houses at the end of the street. Most of the attention, however, focused on 50 Roslyn Court.

Protruding from the bluff face like severed arteries are multicolored, fractured utility lines that served the homes once located on the hillside that has since collapsed. These houses are spectral presences that foretell the future. It was into this landscape of abandonment that I drove one day and saw a For Sale sign planted in front of 50 Roslyn Court. Curious, I stopped and asked a man with a paintbrush in his hand if he was the owner. He couldn't speak English and indicated with hand signals that he was the housepainter. I helped myself to a sheet of paper from the transparent plastic box attached to the sign.

"Panoramic Ocean View!" declared the office-generated sales literature. And, indeed, there was such a view. There were also other enticements. The eighteen-hundred-square-foot home was listed for $789,000 at the height of the most recent real estate boom. It contained three bedrooms and two baths, a two-car garage beneath the living space, granite countertops in the kitchen, and a location close to schools, shopping, and the freeway. There was no mention about the house being on the collapsible edge of a deep pit. So I checked the Web site for the real estate agent, who worked for a nationally recognized firm, and this is what I learned: "It is almost near 50 years since it's built but it's strongly standing on the top of a hill facing Ocean & City."

The agent had the misleading habit of superimposing computer-generated images of that home and another on more spectacular and isolated sites. With the ochre paint barely dry on the two-story home, an open house was scheduled for the next Sunday. I emailed the agent with some questions. He told me the entire Bay Area was subject to earthquakes, the house had stood on that site for fifty years, and the future could not be foretold.

I continued my southward journey. Halfway between Thornton Beach and Mussel Rock there is a gash in the steep bluff known as Avalon Canyon. On one side is the Congregational Christian Church of American Samoa, and on the other is the newer Korean Central Presbyterian Church with its large parking lot. Between the churches is a chain-link fence with a sign reading: Recent Slide Activity, Slide Conditions. Entry Strictly Prohibited. It leads down a steep slope to the outfall for Daly City's questionable storm drain system.

There are three landslide areas within the canyon. One gave way during a December 2003 storm, and 860,000 tons of soil and rocks tumbled into the ocean. Loose rocks and soil continued to fall as workers for a consulting firm hired by the city studied what had happened and what the possible solutions might be. Because of the continuing danger, they could not enter certain areas. The engineers determined, however, that the top of one landslide was subject to "rapid and catastrophic failure without warning" from future earthquakes and storms.[5] The row of Doelger homes that ringed the canyon, and the two churches, were safe, said city officials. In February of 2005 there was another slide on the south flank of Avalon Canyon. The city told residents that acts of nature were to blame.

The coastal drama increases with the greater height of the cliffs towering above nearby Mussel Rock. For thousands of years, gigantic earth slumps caused by seismic activity and coastal storms have consumed these cliffs. The landslides and retreating cliffs created a large U-shaped amphitheater in which there was a sheltered stream and marsh, where Ohlone Indians and early visitors camped during the warmer months. The 1906 State Earthquake Investigation Commission report states, "At the time of the earthquake there was an extensive movement of the landslide, and a tongue of landslide material, about 50 feet high and about 200 feet wide, was projected into the ocean across the narrow strip of beach." All around the bowl "the ground was greatly disturbed by fresh landscape cracks, scarps, and fissures, extending well back from the edge of its encircling cliffs."[6] A few scattered farms dotted the coastal landscape at that time. Now the edges of the amphitheater are crowded with small houses that lie below the flight path of San Francisco International Airport and are shrouded in fog most of the year, making the Daly City coastline one of the most affordable places to live on the edge of the continent for a multiethnic population. There are hidden costs, however. A state geology publication remarks, "Al-most every human enterprise in the Mussel Rock landslide area has been abandoned."[7]

The woes of Daly City homeowners living above Mussel Rock continued after 1906. The land slid in the 1957 and 1989 earthquakes. Runoff from storms hastened the process. As a result, the discontinuous row of homes along the cliff resembles a lower jaw with missing teeth. The problems began when the Doelger builders leveled the top of the bluff by 125 feet in 1960 to create flat homesites. Eleven sites were too close to the bluff and had to be removed from the plans for the subdivision. The solution was simple: dump the earth that had been excavated from the top of the bluff and create eleven pads on unconsolidated ground farther back from the edge. This was done on the west side of the 900 block of Skyline Drive. The results were predictable: five of the houses were soon abandoned, and three lots remained vacant. Doelger bought back some of the homes.

As a temporary measure, Daly City placed plastic sheeting overlaid with dirt over the bare earth to hold back the eroding hillside. However, there was the future to consider. Engineers believe storms and earthquakes will cause a continuing succession of landslides, some much larger than others. "Unfortunately," they believe, "there are no engineering measures that can be reasonably implemented to prevent this from happening."[8]

Where Daly City ends and Pacifica begins, the high bluff gives way to a low coastal terrace and short but steep cliffs leading to the beach. Despite the change in landscapes, there is a litany of repeated coastal disasters. Following the deaths and massive destruction of the 1982 storm, landslides and debris flows occurred with greater frequency. In 1983 a bluff-side trailer park was heavily damaged, despite its armoring with riprap and gunite-coated wooden pilings. The City of Pacifica then undertook a massive coastal armoring project, again to no avail. The ocean kept eating away at the coast. By the time high tides and another intensive storm system descended on Pacifica in early 1998, little was left of the rock revetments. Ten homes on the Esplanade were condemned. A large apartment complex was threatened, and 1.5 miles of coast were again lined with a variety of hardening devices. The reality, however, remained the same: there was no permanent fix for "construction on unstable bluffs that are inexorably receding."[9]

That reality was challenged again just south of Pacifica in 1960. Three years after the debacle of attempting to maintain Highway 1 along the old railroad right-of-way in Daly City ended in abandonment of the problem-plagued roadway, the debate on how best to deal with the recurring closures of the coastal highway at Devil's Slide commenced. Doelger had bought property in Half Moon Bay, a population between one hundred thousand and two hundred thousand people was envisioned, and the immediate solution that leaped to mind was a freeway.

Following tens of thousands of words, hundreds of carefully drawn plans, dozens of lawsuits, and road closures lasting for months, work on twin tunnels, accompanying bridges, and the approaches began in 2005. The tunnel-bridge-roadway widening project serving carbon emitting vehicles will benefit only a handful of commuters in Half Moon Bay, smaller villages to the south, and coastal travelers. The existing highway could have been periodically repaired. There is an alternative inland route leading to many of the same destinations that has been widened over the years to accommodate the increasing traffic from Half Moon Bay to San Francisco and Silicon Valley.

Landslides that periodically block the coast highway and cost millions of dollars to rectify are not confined to the Devil's Slide area. They have occurred wherever roads have been constructed on steep, fragile slopes hovering over the ocean, whether just south of Fort Ross or at Stinson Beach, Big Sur, or Malibu. Drivers want coastal views and ease of access. Caltrans thinks it can impose them and simultaneously maintain a workable angle of repose on hillsides that are prone to periodically collapsing.

The costly highway project at Devil's Slide represented the return to the concept of the 1874 Tobin tunnel. It will contribute to the burgeoning population of Half Moon Bay, once farms but now subdivisions. This bedroom community has its own set of coastal problems. The highest pollution levels of state coastal waters have been recorded at Venice State Beach in Half Moon Bay, and the armoring of the coast extends to a luxury hotel built on the bluffs at the south end of the bay, where the foundation of one structure has already been exposed by the pounding surf.

Complicated odors of fish and antiquity met us as
we entered Monterey, where the street-cars wrought
Anton's nerves to a point of desperation.
J. Smeaton Chase, 1911

THE TOURIST COAST

Monterey, as far as my observation goes, is decidedly
the pleasantest and most civilized-looking place in
California. **Richard Henry Dana Jr., 1835**

Monterey Harbor lies 3 miles southeastward from
Point Pinos, and affords good shelter in southerly
weather. There is a small amount of domestic trade,
general merchandise and lumber being received,
and oil, fish, fruit, and farm products being shipped.
There are two wharves used for commercial
purposes. *United States Coast Pilot,* **1909**

The leading industry of the city today is fishing.
Monterey Bay abounds in sardines (the principal catch),
mackerel, sole, bass, shrimp, squid, crabs, lobsters and
other sea food. Albacore run offshore in spring and late
summer, and further out tuna are caught. Important
by-products are fish meal, fish fertilizer, and fish oils.
The WPA Guide to California, **1939**

This is a monied stretch of coastline—both in terms
of its permanent residents and the life-styles they have
adopted and in what is offered the tourist. There are
shops—mostly in what I think of as the "shoppe"
style—to tempt the buyers in Monterey and Carmel,
whose once-sleepy charm has taken on a pretentious
quaintness. **Philip L. Fradkin,** *California,* **1974**

Today I heard on the radio an interview with a commercial fisherman at Fort Bragg who said that 80 percent of his yearly income had been dependent on the salmon catch; but now, with the sudden collapse of that fishery, he will have to take people out whale watching in order to recover some of his lost income. A restaurant owner on the North Coast—whose customers insist on fresh, local salmon—said in the same interview that, given the loss of salmon and the earlier decline of the lumber industry, the region had become wholly dependent on tourists.

The same could be said of the entire California coast, with the exceptions of residences and businesses in major population centers and the relatively small amounts of acreage devoted to the ports of Eureka, Oakland, Los Angeles, Long Beach, and San Diego. The selling of the coast and its related facilities and amusements to outsiders is now the dominant industry. Catering to strangers began in Monterey, where the concept of luring travelers to an essentially fogbound, chilly, cold-water coast in summer was invented for the benefit of a railroad.

Given Monterey's historical record, what can I tell the fisherman I heard on the radio and others like him? What I can say with some certainty is that, with the careful husbanding of the salmon stock, those fish will return like the populations of sardines, sea otters, elephant seals, and gray whales that were depleted in their times but have since partially recovered. In the meantime, he'd better invest in a fleet of whale-watching vessels, find a job in an aquatic-related tourist attraction, ship as a deckhand on a scientific research vessel, or open up a gift shop specializing in nautical tchotchkes.

The Scottish writer Robert Louis Stevenson lived in Monterey for three months during the fall of 1879, when the town was about to be transformed—by the Southern Pacific Railroad Company and the bulldog tenacity of Charles Crocker—from the decrepit capital of Spanish and Mexican California, and a small American fishing village with dirt streets and wooden sidewalks, into the first large-scale destination and recreation resort on the Pacific Coast. Stevenson took time out from an affair with a married woman, whom he subsequently wedded, to comment upon the local scene. "The one common note of all this country," Stevenson wrote, "is the haunting presence of the ocean." All else was discordant, meaning the straight-laced Methodists in Pacific Grove, the pungent Chinese fishing settlement next door, the "mere bankrupt village" of Monterey just to the east, the predominance of the Spanish language being spoken in the streets, an economy based on credit advanced by "Jew storekeepers," "greedy [Anglo] land-thieves," the ruined Carmel mission, and the forest fires, one of which Stevenson accidentally set when he ignited the lichen hanging on a tree to see if it burned. The following year the "revolution," as Stevenson called it, transformed Monterey.

The Monterey of last year exists no longer. A huge hotel has sprung up in the desert by the railway. Three sets of diners sit down successively to table. Invaluable toilettes figure along the beach and between the live oaks; and

Monterey is advertised in the newspapers, and posted in the waiting-rooms at railway stations, as a resort for wealth and fashion. Alas for the little town! It is not strong enough to resist the influence of the flaunting caravanserai, and the poor, quaint, penniless native gentlemen of Monterey must perish, like a lower race, before the millionaire vulgarians of the Big Bonanza.[1]

Stevenson never returned to Monterey after his brief visit. Like John Steinbeck in the next century, he would trail a myth behind him through Monterey that would greatly benefit the tourist industry. Stevenson was transformed from an arsonist and penniless adulterer into a saintly presence who has a state historical monument and an exclusive private school named after him.

Meanwhile, it took Charlie Crocker of Big Four fame, who had driven Chinese laborers to build the transcontinental railroad across the Sierra Nevada, only one hundred days to construct the looming Gothic/Swiss-chalet style Hotel Del Monte on the outskirts of Monterey. A railroad needed passengers, destinations, land sales, and the control of high-end resorts in order to make money. The Southern Pacific obtained that profitable package when it purchased more than seven thousand acres on the Monterey Peninsula.

Again Chinese laborers were imported, this time to construct what was trumpeted as the "Queen of American Watering Places" and "the handsomest watering-place hotel in America." Luxury, European style, was instantly created on the sand dunes of Monterey Bay. The landscape, as so frequently happens in California, was magically transformed. The

Hotel Del Monte was fantasyland incarnate. The artifice of a European resort contrasted with the crumbling adobes of Monterey.

The hotel's interior comforts and scale matched what guests first saw on the carriage ride from the nearby train depot. There were gardens with exotic plants that suggested a lush Eden or (in the case of cacti) a sere Holy Land; an idyllic lake; a bathing pavilion with a glass ceiling that sheltered four large, heated pools a few hundred feet from the chilly waters of the bay; a polo field and horse-racing track; and, to keep the guests insulated when they left the grounds on horses or in carriages, a carefully crafted and manicured seventeen-mile drive that took them past Chinese and Portuguese fishing villages, through forests, along the rocky seashore, and to the quieter Pebble Beach Lodge and Villas. The first golf course west of the Mississippi was added to the hotel in 1897 and expanded a few years later to eighteen holes. The golf contagion would spread south on the Monterey Peninsula and lead to more scenically spectacular and challenging courses at Pebble Beach and Cypress Point.

A fire destroyed most of the hotel on April 1, 1887. It began in three places at once and was thought to be the work of arsonists, perhaps disgruntled hotel employees. Fires, far more than Stevenson or Steinbeck or the celebrities that flocked to the hotel, were to play an important role in the history of Monterey. The solution to such a disaster, as is often the case in California, was to build as quickly as possible a bigger hotel in the same place that would burn again. Crocker died in his rebuilt hotel the next year, and his corpulent ghost is said to roam the halls of what subsequently became the tony U.S. Naval Postgraduate School.

Not content with creating a fantasyland within the seven thousand acres, the hotel promoters, followed in lockstep by their civic counterparts, altered the Monterey climate to fit what was advertised as "the Riviera of America." Monterey's "vast, wet, melancholy fogs" (Stevenson's words) were transformed by the promoters into a "perennial spring" that lacked a harsh winter or summer, a concept appealing to eastern visitors.[2]

The foggy summer months were passed off as "agreeable" and actually healthy. A visit, or better yet an extended stay at the hotel, was touted as a health cure. The subtle image of a tuberculosis sanitarium, not something every healthy tourist wanted to experience, was evoked by a hotel brochure stating that guests could sit on the veranda, "indolently inhaling the pure air fresh from the ocean." To one doctor, who addressed a Connecticut medical society, "Monterey approaches nearer to the Ideal Sanitarium than any place I know. . . . There is a steady *tone* in the atmosphere which enables and invites you to live out of doors beneath the clear, blue skies, without feeling the enervating effect of the heat further south."[3] For invalids seeking what has become known as alternative medicine, Costanoan Indian cures were offered. Youth could be recovered, it was believed, in the hot springs at nearby Tassajara.

There was money to be made by the railroad from the land. The fine, white sand, whose presence was thought to be inexhaustible because it was replaced daily by the tides and currents, was sold for building purposes, sand blasting, children's sandboxes, and

traps for golf courses. The railroad's subsidiary that oversaw the huge acreage, the Pacific Improvement Company, introduced the concept of expensive housing developments, which exist to this day on the peninsula. The resulting land boom contributed to the identification of the hotel with Monterey. The name *Del Monte* came to dominate the city, just as the Monterey Bay Aquarium, another marine-oriented fantasyland, did when established at the end of the twentieth century. The hotel was built with railroad money, the aquarium with computer money. Both would attract hordes of tourists and serve as models of large-scale coastal developments for their respective eras.

The bridge between hotel and aquarium, what yoked them together across the vagaries of time and history, was fish—specifically their smell. With the odor of drying squid wafting from the Chinese fishing community a nuisance to its Methodist neighbors in Pacific Grove, predominantly Catholic Monterey residents, and to Del Monte Hotel guests to the east, Anglo business interests made attempts to oust the Chinese, which failed until a May 1906 fire destroyed the settlement on what had become known as China Point. The blaze—again, possibly arson—was followed by looting, a pattern established the preceding month in San Francisco's Chinatown. The Chinese refugees, who had fled the San Francisco earthquake to seek safety in the Monterey Chinese settlement, had to move again.

The land belonged to the Pacific Improvement Company, which wanted to move the Chinese and develop the point into a university park. The fire accomplished the company's purposes, and the Southern Pacific land subsidiary offered China Point to the University of California. The deal fell through. The property was then offered to the other Bay Area university. Stanford's Hopkins Marine Station was established on China Point in 1917, thus continuing a scientific presence in Monterey that dated back to 1892, when the West Coast's oldest marine lab was established nearby. Along with tourism, scientific inquiry would eventually prosper in Monterey; but first it was applied to the large-scale mining of fish in offshore waters.

The canneries, first attracted by the salmon and then the sardines, arrived in the early years of the twentieth century. They greatly increased the olfactory effect on the hotel guests and residents of Monterey and Pacific Grove. Monterey's second bard, John Steinbeck, took notice of the pungent odor in *Tortilla Flat*. Citing a changeless quality about Monterey, Steinbeck wrote: "Every day the canneries send a stink of reducing fish into the air."[4] A city odor ordinance, a "smelling committee" known also as "the sniff patrol," and a city inspector were all unable to halt the stink that hung over the area, despite the raging of the hotel's management.

The California sardine, larger than its Atlantic counterpart and known scientifically as *Sardinops caerulea,* was the source of the smell of money that emanated from onshore canneries and "floaters," large ships anchored beyond the three-mile limit to avoid state controls. The prevailing image of the commercial product is of a small headless and tailless silver fish packed in a tight, oily formation and encased in a can with a colorful label. The reality, mean-

ing where most of the money was to be gained from the largest number of sardines, was in the sale of by-products produced by a reduction process. The fish offal was tightly compressed to extract the oil and then baked to produce fertilizer and poultry feed.

It was this process that produced the nauseating odor and the monetary profits that catapulted little Monterey during the first half of the century to its role as the state's and nation's most important fishing port and the world's third largest in terms of tons of industrially processed fish. At its height, and operating in damp, smelly conditions, the sardine industry directly employed 30 to 40 percent of the city's population on an hourly basis when the fish were landed. More than two dozen canneries and reduction plants lined what was then named Ocean View Avenue but would become known as Cannery Row in 1953, in an attempt to reel in tourists with the title of the Steinbeck novel once the sardines had been exhausted.

Two men, Knut Hovden and Ed Ricketts, came to represent an extractive industry and the conservation of a natural resource. Hovden's name is inscribed on the walls of the Monterey Bay Aquarium. Ricketts was immortalized by the writings of his friend Steinbeck. The two men were neighbors on Ocean View.

Knut Hovden was an entrepreneur with a background in fish canning acquired in his native Norway. He arrived in Monterey in 1905, went to work in a cannery, and began improving the technology of canning and extraction to the point where it demanded larger catches. Hovden built his own plant on the site now occupied by the aquarium and began processing sardines in 1916. Sardine production increased twentyfold in Monterey during World War I. The local newspaper declared, "Industrially, Monterey is a fish cannery city; and it is going to be more of a fish cannery city as time goes by."[5]

Hovden's cannery was gutted by fire in 1921, as was his reduction plant in 1924. An arsonist was caught and convicted for the first fire. Hovden thought the second fire was also the work of an arsonist, but there was no proof. It was a bad year for fires in Monterey as the Hotel Del Monte burned for the second time. Once again it was rebuilt on the same site.

With profits from the reduction process growing, Hovden and the other plant owners no longer had to be selective about the size of the catch, since the whole fish could be utilized. An orchestrated dance began, with the scientific staff of the California Department Fish and Game constantly warning of the potential for depletion of the sardines, and the politically appointed fish and game commissioners setting high quotas. "The sardine supply could not be exterminated," declared Hovden, who backed an unsuccessful bond issue to construct an aquarium in 1925.[6]

In the thirty-five years Hovden operated his cannery, he introduced a number of innovations that greatly increased the catch and manufacture of products derived from the sardine. Among them were floating offshore pens into which the catch could be dumped and then sucked into the cannery, a mechanical dryer and cooker, automatic can-capping machines, and larger and more effective nets and vessels. The sardine industry, states a history of the Hovden Cannery commissioned by the Monterey Bay Aquarium Foundation, "benefited more from the work of Knut Hovden than probably that of any other

single person."[7] The opposite was also true: he, along with the industry-dominated state regulators—who wouldn't effectively limit the catch until it was too late—was most responsible for the industry's demise. Hovden's cannery was the last on the row to close, in 1973. The jumble of buildings behind a seawall began to decay, until they were resurrected to net a crop of tourists.

In 1923 Ricketts established his aquatic-related business in Monterey. It consisted of supplying schools and institutions of higher education with marine specimens. A college dropout from Chicago, Ricketts lived a bohemian lifestyle on the fringes, while Hovden was very much ensconced in the midst of Monterey society in a stately home named Trimmer Hill. Ricketts lived amid the hurly-burly of Cannery Row in his two-story wooden Pacific Biological Laboratory, sandwiched between giant metallic cannery buildings and close to Hovden's operation.

Steinbeck's book *Cannery Row*, in which his friend Ricketts is portrayed as the free-spirited Doc, deals with the floaters outside the sardine industry, not the men and women who spent dark nights on the heaving ocean or days amid the clang, dampness, and smell of the canneries and reduction plants. Ricketts was aware of what was going on within the industry, and he became increasingly troubled by it. Far more than a simple collector of specimens, he was an early ecologist who challenged the rigidity of academics and the initial reservations of Stanford University Press to publish *Beyond Pacific Tides,* a textbook and field guide that would be updated through five editions. "It was a view of nature that looked far less like a hierarchical pyramid of species," wrote his biographer, "and far more like an interconnected web of life."[8]

While Ricketts worked in his lab between the picturesquely named Del Vista Packing Company and the Del Mar Canning Company, the sardine industry assiduously pursued the small silver fish whose supply seemed inexhaustible. Ricketts thought otherwise. He amassed statistics on plankton production, sea temperatures, landings, and other relevant factors and studied them carefully in an attempt to understand the declining catches that followed the record hauls during World War II.

No, he said, the cause wasn't the offshore dumping of military explosives, as Hovden claimed in order to take the onus off the sardine industry. The reasons were also more complex than simple overfishing and shifting ocean currents, said Ricketts, although those were part of the equation. The explanations lay somewhere in the labyrinth encompassing human and natural factors, and thus were truly ecological in scope. It was an approach, a present-day scientist said, that was "certainly way before its time."[9]

The Monterey Bay Aquarium seeks to explain the complexities and relationships of intertidal and offshore marine life to the huge number of tourists that visit the city with the sole purpose of a stop at what was once Hovden's cannery. The angled lines of the exterior architecture echo the industrial past. The cannery's boilers and other fixtures have been incorporated into the interior design to emphasize the connection. The aquarium has expanded to abut Ricketts's laboratory, preserved as an anachronistic historic landmark amid the tourist-oriented reincar-

nation of Cannery Row. A mixture of tawdry shops and upscale hotels, restaurants, and spas promise "a new golden age" for the street.[10]

At the apex of the tourist pyramid, the aquarium, like the extravagant hotel and its carefully manicured grounds, is the primary destination that pumps money into the economy of Monterey. A study done for the aquarium states it is "the number one tourist attraction in the area and the principal reason many people visit Monterey."[11] Sybaritic pleasures were the hotel's attractions for the wealthy, while the aquarium's message directed toward a more middle-class clientele is: we will educate you here to be a responsible consumer at home. Serving "ocean-friendly seafood" in the restaurant is one way to achieve this goal.

The hotel and aquarium were and are dependent on luring large numbers of tourists through vigorous promotion of their respective attractions. For the hotel, that meant promoting the concept of a healthy, Mediterranean climate. For the aquarium it means periodically opening a new exhibit space or importing a great white shark or two to drive the attendance upward in order to finance capital improvements, maintenance, and scientific programs. Crowds and income have spiked in those years when the aquarium unveiled new and unusual attractions.

The story of how the aquarium came to be established on the site of the Hovden Cannery has achieved near-legendary status. Friends and members of the family of computer pioneer David Packard brought the idea of an aquarium adjacent to Stanford's Hopkins laboratory to Packard, who was looking for a family project. Packard's daughter Julie, who had a background in marine science, was put in charge. From the beginning the emphasis was on understanding and conserving the regional marine environment. The aquarium could have gone in the more conventional direction of the now-defunct Marineland formerly located on the Palos Verdes Peninsula, and San Diego's Sea World, two aquatic amusement parks, but it didn't. Fifty-five million dollars and countless permits later, the aquarium opened in 1984. Its popularity has exceeded all expectations, and the revenue it has generated surpasses the value of all Monterey Bay sardine catches.

The connections to the past are evident on entering the aquarium. An interpretive sign next to the recreated remnants of Hovden Cannery states: "These boilers were once the heart of a bustling sardine cannery. Today they stand in the heart of an aquarium committed to conserving our oceans." The aquarium also lays claim to the legacy of Ed Ricketts. A booklet available in the store states that "the aquarium's unique exhibit approach showcasing regional marine communities rather than individual species was influenced" by Ricketts.[12]

One of those communities is the kelp forest. The most anthropomorphic creature inhabiting kelp beds, or for that matter ocean waters, is the California sea otter. The otter has become the poster child for the marine environment. A photograph of a small, cuddly otter adorns the cover of the aquarium's publication *Monterey Bay Aquarium: The Insider's Guide*. When I visited the aquarium, banners on the street outside the massive structures, which cover three acres, proclaimed the current hit exhibit, Wild About Otters. Like attendance at the aquarium, the annual

count of sea otters has leveled off. Pathogens from kitty litter and sewage dumped into the ocean have been blamed.

The strength of the Monterey Bay Aquarium lies in the fact that, unlike the basement aquarium in the new California Academy of Sciences in Golden Gate Park, it lies adjacent to the environment it depicts. Future tourist attractions could very well lie just offshore. In fact, the Monterey aquarium has been progressing in that direction. In the sandy seafloor tank of the Monterey Bay Exhibit, I saw flat Dover sole lying disguised on the silt-laden bottom while bright orange starfish were quite visible. A flowerlike tube anemone seized plankton drifting by on the current. Upstairs in the tiny drifter section of the Outer Bay Exhibit, dense swirls of snowflakelike plankton sailed past like miniature cottonwood seeds in the breeze. There were krill, larval crabs, diatoms, dinoflagellates, and tiny translucent jellies within the mass. These two exhibits came closest to mimicking life-forms in bay waters. A journey into the depths was depicted on live television feeds from whatever research vessel was working offshore at the time, and a room was filled with computer simulations showing how the vessel operated.

The scientific legacies of the Hopkins and Ricketts laboratories; the extraordinary popularity of the aquarium, and its emphasis on conservation and research; and Californians' custom of doing things on a massive scale—like building luxury hotels, large canneries, and innovative aquariums—have led to the creation of a marine research community numbering two dozen institutions and the establishment of marine protected areas surrounding Monterey.

Nature has provided a rich and varied marine environment ranging from the intertidal zone to the nearby two-mile depths. The result is that the seafloor off Monterey is the best-observed marine habitat in the world.

In order to gain a sense of what the offshore region resembled, a glimpse at the aquarium's research activities, and a close look at the Monterey Bay National Marine Sanctuary, Alex and I departed early one August morning on the *Point Lobos,* a research vessel belonging to the Monterey Bay Aquarium Research Institute (MBARI). David Packard had established the institute on the edge of the bay and miles from the madding crowds at the aquarium in order to bring engineers, scientists, and operating staff together to search the ocean off California in a manner similar to how space is probed. MBARI is a miniature NASA of the depths that operates on private funds. Both dispatch complicated machinery to unfamiliar places.

On this morning a dense fog was settled over the harbor at Moss Landing and the outside bay, obscuring the major landmark: the tall stacks of the oil-burning power plant that had been spewing carbon dioxide into the air since the early 1950s and had only recently been converted to burning natural gas. The vessel's daylong trip was part of a study to determine the effects of fossil fuels on marine organisms. That meant tracing the cycle of carbon dioxide that increased the acid content of ocean water ingested by marine life. While the effect of fossil fuels on the atmosphere, and the resulting global warming, has been extensively studied, little is known about fossil fuels' effect on the oceans, which absorb one-third of the carbon dioxide emitted yearly.

The past was present as we slowly glided through the harbor. It was sardine season, and the half-dozen sardine boats using Moss Landing as their home port were docked after a night's work. The seals and sea lions that covered all bare dock space in the harbor, and that were numerous in the surrounding waters, indicated the sardines had returned. Fishermen and the organizations representing them were chafing at state-imposed limits on catches. No sardines landed at Moss Landing or Monterey, however, were processed there. They were shipped frozen around the world.

The 110-foot *Point Lobos,* named after a spectacular, rocky outcrop south of Carmel, and the *Ventana,* the remotely operated vehicle (ROV) painted bright orange that bore the name of a nearby wilderness area, began life in the oil industry. They underwent major alterations after being acquired by the institute. The *Ventana* was the workhorse of the institute's fleet of ROVs, which was at sea more than three hundred days a year. The ungainly vehicle bristling with remotely controlled arms, lights, cables, television cameras, and all manner of electronics would dive three times on this day, making a grand total of 3,256 submersions in its lifetime up to that point.

The *Ventana* was joined to the mothership by a thick tether containing fiber optic and power cables. It would be dropped on the edge of the Monterey Canyon to depths of 425 and 860 feet and at distances of 5 and 10 miles from shore. Its mission was to recover tube-shaped benthic respirators that measure carbon consumption, collect two samples of sediment, and scoop up 350 brachiopods, which were being used as an indicator species. More commonly known as lampshells, the brachiopods look like clams. They have been around for a long time. Some 250 million years ago they just barely survived the Permo-Triassic event, the worst mass extinction of all time. This study and others were trying to head off just such a catastrophe.

When the *Point Lobos* reached the first station, a crane gently lifted the expensive piece of machinery off the deck and deposited it gently in the slight swells of Monterey Bay. The *Ventana*'s propulsion system took over, and it slowly sank. Below the forward deck of the *Point Lobos* was a control room with enough screens to resemble the television sales room of a big box store. The high-definition images revealed minute details of the underwater world as the ROV descended. "Incredible visibility today," someone muttered. The work, demanding great concentration and precision, was done to the accompaniment of country music.

There were long interludes of floating plankton passing by the cameras. Alex thought it was like driv-ing in a snowstorm. The crew called it marine snow. Then delicate, bioluminescent creatures would swim past the camera. They included a bullet-shaped ctenophore, or comb jelly, its beating cilia reflecting rainbow colors as the lights of the ROV briefly caught it and the camera recorded the momentary image. A small version of a siphonophore known as nanomia, whose tail was lit like a string of undulating Christmas lights, swam into view. A more dangerous species was the Portuguese man-of-war. Some species of siphonophores reach lengths of 130 feet, making them the longest animals in the world.

We returned, and Alex and I had a fish dinner that night at a popular local restaurant, where the owner told us "it all began with sardines" and related that, as a boy, he had gone longline fishing with his grandfather in Monterey Bay. I recalled our previous boat trip thirty-five years ago, when Alex and I had accompanied a California Fish and Game crew to the water off the then-nonexistent aquarium to tag sea otters. The small, towheaded boy with freckles had got to hold a baby sea otter while the mother otter was tagged.

Facing Santa Monica Bay from a high mesa is Santa Monica (100 alt., 37,146 pop.), a residential-resort city with a substantial business center, whose summer visitors swell the population figure to more than 100,000. . . . Venice (20 alt., 19,260 pop.) [is] an ocean-front pleasure town with an elaborate amusement section on the beach and pier. A flying circus, giant dipper, bamboo slide, and rolling barrels are among the devices that have given Venice the title "Coney Island of the West." **The WPA Guide to California, 1939**

THE RECREATIONAL COAST

At the end of the sand dunes on the south side of Ballona Lagoon is Playa del Rey and on the north side of the lagoon is Venice; Ocean Park is one mile southeastward from Santa Monica and there are two piers at the latter place. None of these piers are used by vessels nor for commercial purposes. **United States Coast Pilot, 1909**

Traffic separation lanes have been established in the entrance channel to Marina del Rey. These lanes are marked by State Waterway Regulatory Buoys with the words "No Sail." All vessels under power, or power and sail, shall keep these buoys to their port when entering or departing the harbor. The center lane between the buoys is used by vessels solely under sail, both entering and departing the harbor. **United States Coast Pilot, 2006**

"Let's go to the beach!" Millions of people heed that happy call each year and go to Los Angeles County beaches. Recreation is the most common connection California residents have with the coastline. Nowhere else along the shoreline is the recreational experience more massive, intense, or varied, or dramatized more extensively, than at the adjoining beach communities of Santa Monica, Venice, and Marina del Rey.

A population exceeding ten million, a year-round temperate climate, warm water, long stretches of sandy beaches, and proximity to the television and movie industries have made Los Angeles beaches among the most heavily used and extensively popularized in the world. For more than one hundred years, the beaches have provided extreme pleasures in countless forms for millions of people. When J. Smeaton Chase passed this way on his 1911 journey up the coast, he made a detour to avoid the crowds and, by his choice of route, gave credence to the popularity of the beach communities at that time. "I was willing to forego the sight of that galaxy of seashore pleasure towns," Chase wrote, "which, in the exuberant metaphor of real estate circulars, 'are flung like a tribute of gems at the feet of imperial Los Angeles.' "[1]

The city and its immediate environs are image prone beyond the norm. History is a shallow concept in Southern California, and what past there is retreats quickly like diminishing time-lapse images that fade to nothing. There is no greater contemporary Left Coast image than the one that matches perfect bodies with perfect sand and perfect salt water. Behind the mythic representations, there is a Dionysian history of pleasure seeking—and a gritty reality.

From Point Conception south to the Mexican border—and nowhere more noticeably than at Los Angeles County beaches—the air and water differ from what is found to the north. Where the land suddenly jogs ninety degrees to the east, the offshore Channel Islands buffer the Pacific swells, sandy beaches become more prevalent, and the cold California current shoots directly south and away from the land to be replaced by a warmer inshore current and more constant sun. The semicircle extending south to the border known as the Southern California Bight has attracted most of the state's population, which huddles as close as possible to a seemingly benign ocean.

In stark contrast to the vast changes that have occurred to the south, Point Conception is one of the few places where very little has been altered since Richard Henry Dana sailed past in the brig *Pilgrim* in early 1835. It was smooth sailing to the south, but heavy going to the north. Dana wrote, "This is the largest point on the coast, and it is an uninhabited headland, stretching out into the Pacific, and has the reputation of being very windy."[2] The *Coast Pilot* refers to the point as the "Cape Horn of the Pacific" because of heavy winter gales and summer fogs.[3]

There is a softer climate to the south. The light differs here; absent are the sharper outlines, greater clarity of details, and more vivid colors found north of Point Conception. A diaphanous curtain is lowered over the landscape on most days. In a 1998 California issue, the *New Yorker* magazine devoted an entire story to the distinct quality of light in Los Angeles, repeating some of the same points made in 1946 by Carey McWilliams, whose articles and books remain the best histories and descriptions of what he called "an island on the land." McWilliams caught the essence of the light and the reality of the place before the years of serious smog. Of the proximity of the ocean to the desert he writes, "When the sunlight is not screened and filtered by the moisture-laden air, the land is revealed in all its semi-arid poverty."[4]

Once the morning fog has lifted, that special light bathes the seaside communities of Santa Monica, Venice, and Marina del Rey and partially obscures their differences by its sameness. Nowhere else along the coast have three adjoining communities pursued beachside pleasures so relentlessly in ways that have attracted such dissimilar crowds. In the order that I noticed them offshore from a speeding Baywatch boat manned by a Los Angeles County lifeguard captain, the look-alike squat apartments and condominiums of Marina del Rey gave way to the irregular, gap-toothed skyline of Venice and then the orderly whiteness of Santa Monica, where high-rises dominated the bluff like gleaming missiles readied for launching.

Santa Monica, or rather the tents pitched in the late nineteenth century in Santa Monica Canyon before the city was established, was where the Southern California beach scene began. With the completion of the Santa Monica Pier in 1909, what had become a small village gained its popular beach identity, which it has retained to the present. Santa Monica would be nothing without its wide, sandy beach and ease of access—first by horseback and wagon, then by railroad and trolley, and later by automobile on dirt paths, the two-lane Highway 66, and finally the multilane Santa Monica Freeway. All converged on the pier, which gained iconic status over the years.

Another constant has been water pollution. The primary purpose of the original sixteen-hundred-foot pier was to dump the town's sewage beyond the line of surf and into quieter ocean waters. A storm drain beneath the pier now contributes to the surrounding beach's status as one of the most polluted in the state. A study of gastroenteritis at Southern California beaches determined that "Santa Monica, the beach with the highest attendance, has the highest excess GI [gastrointestinal illnesses] of all beaches during the wet and dry seasons."[5]

"Magneto-electrolytic" treatment of the sewage and a unique all-concrete pier that would supposedly defy "the ravages of time" put the city on the road to progress in 1909, it was thought. Five years later the city was looking into the possibility of constructing a seawall in the ocean so the raw sewage would not wash ashore and ruin the bathing. Ten years later the concrete pilings were cracking and portions of the pier were sinking. Four hundred and eighty creosote-soaked wooden pilings were driven into the sand. Santa Monica would eventually send its sewage to the Hyperion Sewage Treatment Plant to the south, which has had its own pollution problems.[6]

With its new municipal pier, Santa Monica was launched on a limited trajectory toward furnishing a vast number of diverse people with pleasure. In addition to its primary function, the pier was also a magnet for bathing, provided a platform from which to fish, and was a promenade. Piers, and there were many of them in Southern California during the first half of the twentieth century, are places where poor people without yachts or the means to pay for an ocean passage can enjoy a sense of being on the water.

The elusive quality of life known as pleasure was vastly increased with construction of an adjoining 1,055-foot pier in 1916 that received the official designation of "pleasure pier." A carousel, roller coaster, and huge ballroom were grafted onto the main pier. The Hippodrome, still present with its distinctive conical roof, housed successive merry-go-rounds. The latest carousel was salvaged from a 1947 fire on the Venice Beach Pier. Fires, along with storms and constant shifts in the popularity of entertainments, such as the rise of inland Disneylands, took their toll on the many pleasure piers in Southern California, until only the dual Santa Monica piers remained.

There were other problems with the piers, such as occasional accidental drownings and intentional suicides and the question of how to keep the "spooners" out from underneath the piers at night. One night watchman complained of having to patrol for "loving couples" among the dank, barnacle-encrusted pilings. There were periodic reports of sea serpents. Offshore lights from fishing boats during World War I panicked seaside residents into thinking German warships were offshore. The salty manager of the pier stated, "Any fool son of a wall-eyed sea cook should have sense enough to know that no enemy boat would be showing lights if she was intending mischief here."

Periodically, about every ten or fifteen years, the amusements needed upgrading to keep the crowds coming. This meant a series of new roller coasters and other rides and amusements. There was no greater upgrade than the construction of a gigantic auditorium. Professor La Monica and the Royal Italian Band played concerts and dance music on the open pier. The bandleader was credited with having more colorful uniforms than any other conductor in the country. He lent his name to the La Monica Ballroom, whose exterior was described as modified Spanish stucco with an interior dash of French renaissance. This hulking, turreted edifice was suspended on spindly legs over the Pacific Ocean. It was hailed as the world's biggest ballroom, Southern California being the world's leader in the use of superlatives to describe its attractions.

If not the largest, then perhaps it was the gaudiest. Thirty-six bell-shaped chandeliers suspended from gold ropes hung above the interior promenade that surrounded the fifteen-thousand-square-foot dance floor. Fourteen thousand strips of maple cut in lengths of sixteen feet were laid in complex patterns to break up the monotony of the huge space. Don Clark was the leader of the La Monica Orchestra when the ballroom was dedicated in 1924 "to the pleasure of thousands" in front of a crowd estimated the next day at twenty-five thousand by the local newspaper, a constant booster of the pier. A variety of uses occurred in the immense structure over the years: it became a site for walking and dance marathons, a convention center, a private club for University of Southern California alumni, a roller-skating rink, an automobile museum, a police department and city jail, a lifeguard headquarters, and a location for movie and television show sets.

The inevitable was not long in coming. Large waves from a storm pounded the pier, and the fishing fleet took refuge where it could find it. In early 1926 another storm damaged the ballroom and tore away part of the municipal pier's boat landing. Two months later the captain of the "pleasure fishing business" and two of his crewmen were drowned trying to save a boat in a storm. It should have been apparent then that pain inevitably accompanies pleasure, especially when manmade piers are extended into perilous waters. But one month later, in May, plans were submitted for a breakwater off the end of the pier that would supposedly shelter the structure and moored vessels.

The popularity of dancing waned in the depression years. In 1932, when work on the breakwater finally began after legislative and funding delays, Santa Monica was pinning its economic hopes on attracting the yachting crowd, as Los Angeles County would thirty years later with the construction of Marina del Rey. It was thought that film people such as Louis B. Mayer would keep their yachts behind a secure breakwater, and a first-of-its-kind breakwater would herald a new, prosperous era for the city by the sea.

The problem was that concrete was once again used to build an underwater structure. The concrete cribs designed to contain rocks and boulders cracked under the strain. Stone was substituted for the entire breakwater. Boulders from a quarry on Santa Catalina Island weighing ten tons were used to cap the pyramid-shaped structure in early 1934, and the yacht harbor was dedicated in August. With the first storms in October, the breakwater needed repairs, and more stones were dumped on the structure.

There were also problems onshore. The pier and new breakwater trapped sand, widening the Santa Monica beach while diminishing the sand-starved beaches to the south. But Santa Monica was doing just fine, thank you. Hollywood celebrities came and went on boats, a record beach crowd of one hundred thousand was estimated on one hot June day, and Muscle Beach, just south of the pier, was attracting crowds of physical fitness buffs and the curious to ogle the physiques of Jack LaLanne, Joe Gold, and other muscle-bound exhibitionists.

By 1940 the breakwater was judged a failure because it trapped too much sand, and expensive dredging could not keep up with the constant need to deepen the channel. It was feared that storm surges would batter the seawall into submission and damage the main pier, as they eventually did. The city engineer warned: "Pilings and timbers would go adrift, and the entire pier might be reduced to a log jam which could batter and sink every boat in the harbor." Meantime, the pier's businesses donated to the city a neon-lighted sign spanning the entrance to the pier. It advertised a yacht harbor with sportfishing and boating. The quaint sign stands to this day—minus a harbor—as a symbol for vanished recreational opportunities. A line of white buoys warns boaters away from the former breakwater, which has been reduced to a crumbling replica of an unplanned artificial reef.

World War II brought its share of scares and a nighttime curfew on the beach but not the pier. A new owner of the pleasure pier took over, vowing great improvements. Johnny Weissmuller, a movie Tarzan and the winner of five Olympic swimming gold medals, was sunning on the beach when he heard a boy in the water yelling for help. He beat lifeguards to the boy and saved him from drowning. With the pier threatened in 1945 by the proposed removal of the breakwater, the question was: what would Santa Monica have left in the way of beach identity if the pier was destroyed by waves? Not much, really.

The deteriorating La Monica Ballroom, where the "King of Western Swing," Spade Cooley, and his band held their weekly television shows after the war, was the first to go. By the late 1960s, the city owned both piers. A plan was submitted in 1971 to raze the piers and create a thirty-acre artificial offshore island complete with multistory hotels, amusements, and whatever else would produce income for the city on a vulnerable islet. It is difficult to perceive now how such a plan could even have been considered, let alone be approved by the city council. Yet both actions took place. The inevitable "Save the Pier" citizens' group was organized. The fight was bitter. Santa Monica's own Robert Redford was filming *The Sting* with Paul Newman on the pier at the time. As a boy he had fished from the pier and ridden the carousel. "It was fun," he recalled. The pier was saved, and the city councilmen who had supported its demolition were voted out of office.

The pier had become Santa Monica. The architectural critic Reyner Banham wrote in 1971: "One can see the pier as the seed or trigger which has precipitated the whole development of Santa Monica" as Southern California's first resort city.[7] In fact, said Banham, the pier was the initial reason why the city was founded. The architectural firm of Frank O. Gehry & Associates was hired in 1975 to produce yet another restoration plan. Nothing was done. Then in 1983 a series of late January El Niño storms battered the Southern California coast, causing widespread damage to shoreline structures whose owners thought they were immune from danger and had crowded too close to the seemingly placid ocean. One third of the west end of the pier was damaged and the tip was missing, along with a restaurant and the harbormaster's office.

The mayor, having absorbed the earlier political lesson, declared that the pier was the "heart and symbol" of Santa Monica. Seven years later the latest restoration of the pier was completed. The usual celebration complete with marching bands, jazz concerts, free carousel rides for children, and fireworks brought the crowds back to the venerable structure. The pleasure pier was leased to a corporate entity named Pacific Park, who again upgraded the amusement facilities. Gone were the old-fashioned bumper cars Alex and I had crashed into each other in the early seventies and the simple Ferris wheel my daughter, Cleo, and I had ridden fifteen years later. The new Ferris wheel had 160,000 computer-controlled LED lights flashing in vivid combinations at night.

Not much had really changed when I revisited the pier with Alex. As usual, large crowds had trooped to Los Angeles County beaches on a late July weekend. The pier scene resembled a teeming carnival on water. Screams of delight and fear emanating from the thrill rides, jammed strollers wandering aimlessly, and the packed strip of sunbathers with multicolored umbrellas and Styrofoam coolers huddling as close as possible to the line of surf testified to the continuing pleasure of going to the beach.

There was, however, one startling anomaly located in the dry sand adjacent to the north side of the pier. Over four thousand simple white crosses stood in precise rows that contrasted markedly with the milling crowds surrounding them. They were a memorial to servicemen and -women killed in Iraq and Afghanistan. There were signs stating that more than forty-five hundred had been killed, sixty thousand injured, and one million civilian casualties suffered since March 2003. A record had been established that week. There had been no military deaths in Iraq, although five servicemen had died in Afghanistan.

The mournful tune of "Taps" played continuously over a loudspeaker at what the Veterans for Peace called Arlington West, while the public came and went with more immediate concerns on its mind. Arriving beachgoers detoured around the crosses with blinders on. They were intent on finding their spaces on the crowded sand. Departing beachgoers paused at the shower adjacent to the display. They were intent on washing off beach sand.

A small boy suddenly darted from the shower and beat the sand next to a cross with his fist.

"Is he right here, Dad?"

"No, no," was the father's reply, with no further elaboration.

I couldn't think of a more powerful public display of the human costs of waging a war and the lack of any sacrifices on the part of a civilian population than the startling juxtaposition of these two very American scenes. War was on my mind because I hadn't seen or heard so many helicopters in one place since my time in Vietnam as a newspaper correspondent. Some were private craft; most that cruised just off-shore from Santa Monica to Marina del Rey were dedicated to some type of public safety. The constant beating of noisy rotors made relaxation, let alone napping on the beach, impossible for me.

Then there was the unpleasant matter of water quality that week at local beaches. Indications of sewage were detected and warning signs of pollution were in place at the end of Topsail Street in Venice, at the end of Wilshire Boulevard in Santa Monica, and on both sides of the pier. On the weekly report card issued by Heal the Bay, the pier ranked at the top of the list of Santa Monica Bay beaches exceeding bacteria limits, with seventy violations since April 1. The pier was also at the top of the list of beaches with the greatest number of violations that could result in fines of ten thousand dollars a day. Two other Santa Monica beaches were among the top eight on that particular list.

A 1995 study of fecal coliform counts at three Santa Monica beaches was the first such large-scale report with national implications that indicated there were health risks for people who swam near storm drains that disgorged urban runoff, mainly during the rainy winter months. We were there during the dry season when supposedly no flows of bacteria-laced pollutants were making their way from storm drains to the ocean. But water with high fecal bacteria counts was still present in the sand surrounding a stagnant pond under the pier where "sky high" bacteria levels were measured.[8] Supposedly, a solution was in the works, just as it had been in 1909.

How many beachgoers had suffered ill effects, and what were the direct costs? Beaches in Los Angeles and Orange counties, which have attracted more than

26. *(Previous page)* Early white settler homestead ruins near site where Native Americans were massacred. Bear Harbor, Lost Coast, 2009.

27. Marina following path through a burned forest. Big Sur, 2008.

28. Dad and old growth redwood forest. Prairie Creek Redwoods State Park, 2007.

29. Flag in field. Mendocino County, 2009.

30. Three surfers viewing wave conditions. Venice Beach, 2008.

31. Santa Monica Beach, Iraq-Afghanistan War Memorial, and pier. Santa Monica, 2008.

32. *(Above)* Casino. Klamath River, 2009.

33. *(Right)* "Wooden Indian" with no face. Ocean Beach, San Francisco, 2008.

34. *(Above)* Cannon porthole aimed out to sea. Fort Point, San Francisco, 2007.

35. *(Right)* Tunnel access to Gun Battery 129. Fort Baker, Marin Headlands, 2009.

36. (*Above*) The original Gold's Gym, where Arnold Schwarzenegger was filmed in *Pumping Iron,* now a remodeled upscale residence. Venice Beach, 2007.

37. (*Right*) Obama "Hope" poster hanging in the window of Frank Gehry's Venice Beach House. Venice Beach, 2007.

38. Treasure hunter with metal detector under the Santa Monica Pier. Santa Monica, 2006.

39. Overgrown ruins of Clayton Lewis's home. Lairds Landing, Tomales Bay, 2006.

40. World War II spotting station disguised as a farmhouse. Klamath, 2008.

41. Shopping cart and wall mural of agricultural scene. Watsonville, 2010.

42. Abandoned homes in old lumber town. Samoa, near Eureka, 2009.

43. *(Previous spread)* RVs camped on beach. Oceano Dunes, 2007.

44. *(Right)* Family and their little red truck on beach. Pismo Beach, 2007.

45. Danger, Sheer Unstable Cliffs. Sunset Cliffs, San Diego, 2010.

46. Illuminated bridge and shipping cranes. Long Beach, 2007.

47. Plastic bottle, bull kelp, and tar stains on rocks. Point Lobos, Carmel, 2008.

48. Josh on ATV. Oceano Dunes, 2007.

49. *(Right)* Marina's legs and Che. Gold Bluffs Beach, Humboldt County, 2008.

50. *(Following page)* Cargo containers being off-loaded, and detail of ship's bow. Port of Los Angeles, San Pedro, 2009.

eighty million people in a year, have caused, according to one study, between 628,000 and 1,400,000 gastrointestinal illnesses, resulting in healthcare costs with an annual range between $21 million and $51 million.

With Santa Monica Bay beaches among the most polluted in the state, I decided not to go swimming that week. Alex did, and suffered no ill effects.

I associate Venice with feet, specifically the sound of thousands of feet encased in flip-flops plop, plop, plopping along on Ocean Front Walk, and with feet balanced on the polyethylene wheels of roller skates and inline blades. I suppose the sound of soft foam hitting hard concrete and the noise of what propels people on skates are a strange way to envision this diverse beachfront community, but a writer needs to follow his instincts and see where they lead him.

First, the sandals, which can be generic and cheap or fashionably trendy and expensive. They are present in abundance, are convenient footwear for shuffling along on Ocean Front Walk, and are associated with sand, beaches, warm weather, and informality, all ingredients of the mythic Southern California beach scene. In the communities immediately to the north and south of Venice, I noted fewer flip-flops and more formal footwear.

The invention of the polyethylene wheel for skates in the 1970s launched Venice on a trajectory toward becoming a vibrant coastal community after its first incarnation and subsequent demise as a real estate set for its Italian namesake city at the beginning of the last century. First there had been sand dunes, then an extravaganza of amusements and canals and quaintly arched bridges and Venetian gondoliers, followed by a dense forest of oil wells, shacks, beachfront hotels, and Craftsman cottages, three piers, urban decay, and what became increasingly rare in Los Angeles County, an inexpensive place to live near the beach for free spirits and staid souls during the bohemian and hippie years.

For pedestrians and bike riders, first there had been the straight course of Ocean Front Walk and the possibility of collisions. Then an undulating eighteen-mile concrete bike path was constructed parallel to beachfront streets from Torrance to Santa Monica in 1972 to accommodate the ten-speed-bike fad. By the middle of the decade the polyurethane wheel had been invented and installed on roller skates, enabling a more stable ride for skaters on the path. The new wheel also accounted for the return of skateboarding, moribund since the mid-1960s. The innovative style of the Z-Boys (and one girl), who surfed in the morning and skateboarded in the afternoon on the beaches and inclines of Santa Monica and Venice, attracted more board and wheel converts. They hung out at a surf shop in Dogtown on the border of the two beachfront communities. Their emphasis on a low-slung style and extreme acrobatics, whether on the water or on the concrete, influenced surfing and skateboarding, two quintessential California sports with overlapping subcultures that sprouted and then spread from these communities.

The wheeled crowds converged on Venice and began transforming the depressed community. They either stumbled along with plenty of protective gear or executed balletic turns with precision, grace, and rhythm. The crowds watching the stunts attracted street vendors, new businesses in old structures, street performers, bodybuilders (when Muscle Beach moved south from Santa Monica, and Gold's Gym opened in Venice), tattoo artists, mural painters, musicians, and fortune-tellers. Venice was declared "the roller skating capital of the world," and the Z-Boys became a momentary phenomenon enshrined on the screen and in numerous publications.

The 1984 Los Angeles Olympics brought national and international attention through television to the rejuvenated community, which *Sunset* magazine later declared to be second only to Disneyland in visitor appeal. The wheeled fads continued, and included inline skates, scooters, mountain bikes, and cruiser bikes. All means of leg-powered propulsion are represented today on the path in an eclectic and perhaps world-record mix.

Along the way something different from other California beach communities evolved in Venice, something related to its self-perceived role as a model of social and economic tolerance and diversity. As a rule, California beach communities are not diverse. It takes money—lots of money in most cases—to live next to or near the water. In Venice, with scattered exceptions, the rich don't live on the ocean's edge— the homeless and middle class do. Strolling tourists and vendors occupy Ocean Front Walk during the day. In the evening hours the homeless arrive pushing their overloaded shopping carts. With a nudge from the police, they disappear early the next morning only to return that evening like conventional commuters. Instead of behind gates, the rich live in fortresslike structures interspersed between shabby apartments and cottages. The trendy shops and res-

taurants are inland along Abbot Kinney Boulevard.

One of the more renowned street performers delivered the Venice message on a Sunday afternoon at the center of the beach scene at Windward Passage and Ocean Front Walk. Alex Bartlette, a native of Saint Kitts, was the leader of the Calypso Tumblers. His five fellow tumblers warmed up the crowd for the main event, which featured Bartlette.

But first came the sermon. "If you want your mother, father, teacher to be proud of you, don't mess with drugs or alcohol," lectured Bartlette with a Caribbean lilt to his English. "It's not good. Remember, it's only one race, the human race, and that's why we should learn, people, to live together and be more civilized." Bartlette's five fellow tumblers, acting as a chorus, echoed his last words in unison.

"Is everyone ready? I'm a trained professional." The chorus chanted mockingly, "That's why he works the streets."

To the tumblers, and to the volunteers drawn hesitantly from the crowd, all of whom were bent over in a row, Bartlette issued a command: "Touch your toes, put your heads down, don't move. If you move, you die." The six children who had been recruited were effectively frozen in place. To the crowd of two hundred, he said: "If you want to see it, clap." The clapping built in crescendo, much like a drum roll.

The lithe Bartlette, with the same grace and insouciance as an expert surfboarder or skateboarder, backed up, took a long run, flipped once in the air, narrowly cleared the bent figures, and landed running on his feet, to instant applause. He shamed the crowd into giving more generously than it normally would have by pointing out that one dollar meant only twenty cents per tumbler. Five and ten dollar bills piled up in the orange plastic buckets the tumblers passed among the dispersing crowd as wisps of fog crossed the beach near the end of another summer weekend.

Santa Monica is a relatively staid community; Venice is a mixed community; Marina del Rey is a transient community. Of course, all three contain elements of the others, and all three are completely dependent upon the ocean and beach for their economic survival. The communities did not shape the natural environment; the shoreline shaped them, a seemingly self-evident truth that gets lost in the commercial hustle. If pleasure is derived from an amusement park in Santa Monica and the motion of legs in Venice, then small boats and large yachts are the means for extracting fun, along with huge amounts of money, in Marina del Rey.

Means is a keyword, because watercraft are the means for raising large amounts of revenue for the County of Los Angeles. The marina has been characterized as being the county's "largest cash-producing asset" and its "most valuable single resource."[9] Larger boats in bigger slips; bigger hotels and taller office buildings; more high-rise condos and squat apartments; and costlier retail shops and restaurants are the policies that are driving the hoped-for rejuvenation of the marina, which is less than fifty years old and thus an ancient presence in this land of the enduring present.

What became the marina and the home for gleaming multimillion-dollar megayachts and more modest plastic-hulled sailboats was originally the terminus for the Los Angeles River and what was considered valueless marshland. The wild, uncontrolled surges of the river, before it was encased in concrete, bounced back and forth across the Los Angeles Plain, sometimes settling on Ballona Creek as its outlet to the ocean. The central plain was awash at times. Duck hunters walked or rowed across Ballona Marsh, from which the marina would be carved. Then came the oil fields in the 1930s. The flat marshland next attracted the aviation pioneer Howard Hughes, who established his aircraft factory and airstrip during World War II near what would become the marina.

Long envisioned as a major commercial harbor and then as a recreational boating center, the wetland began being transformed into a small-craft marina in 1957. It was dedicated in 1965 as the largest manmade recreational harbor serving small craft in the world, and it may still be that, because the marina in Dubai in the United Arab Emirates has not yet reached Marina del Rey's capacity for holding forty-five hundred vessels. Rather than a boat harbor, however, the marina—referred to locally as The Marina—has become more a state of mind, or rather the imagination. The eight hundred acres that compose the marina, almost evenly divided between land and water, are promoted as the hip, hot, and cool place to be: "a cutting-edge city" within a city. Tellingly, in terms of population demographics, there are no schools within the marina. It is a very specialized community.

The boat basin designed to lure land-based revenue producers began rather disastrously. The U.S. Army Corps of Engineers constructed two parallel rock breakwaters into the ocean that unwittingly served as a trough for incoming waves. In the winter of 1962–1963, tropical storms off Mexico generated large swells that rolled north and entered the channel, setting up huge surges within the marina that wrecked the new docks and the first moored boats. The marina, then a flat expanse of fill land, partially dissolved under the onslaught.

It was not an auspicious beginning. The corps studied the problem and came up with the solution of a third breakwater offshore that would act as a cap on the two parallel breakwaters, with room for boats to depart and enter on the sides. The wasteland was landscaped, leased, and developed; and everything functioned fairly smoothly until the 1990s, when the county put pressure on the aging marina to produce more income.

The California Coastal Commission held hearings ten years later and determined that the marina, where it was possible to be married on the water and buried at sea, along with all the customary onshore amenities, no longer served its primary purpose as a recreational boating facility. Fewer boat slips, which allowed for additional land-based developments, and the enlarging of existing slips for bigger and wider boats was one indication that the Los Angeles County Department of Beaches and Harbors had money mainly on its mind.

When Alex and I visited the marina, the evidence for that conclusion was evident in an extreme form. Tied up at the gas dock—because no other dock was long enough to accommodate it—was the gleaming white megayacht *Princess Mariana* owned by the Mexican telecom mogul Carlos Slim Helú, then the second-richest man in the world. The 252-foot vessel

named for Helú's wife had six decks and included a carport and base for support vessels that entered the mothership, much like smaller spacecraft docked at the starship *Enterprise*. On the topmost deck there was a helipad with a helicopter. When the chopper was absent, the pad became a golf driving range where balls were aimed at a giant screen depicting the famous golf courses of the world. There was a swimming pool, dance floor, gym, cinema, and six staterooms. The floating palace cost $650,000 to charter for one week.

In an era and a country that were ripe for economic puncturing, the megayacht was a fitting symbol of the great disparity between wealth and poverty and a clear indication to me that something drastic was about to occur. The white yacht represented the excesses that were about to cause the great recession that followed shortly after our visit to Marina del Rey. The vessel remained docked for the week in late July 2008 when we monitored its presence. It attracted gawkers who venerated the great wealth it represented. They hung on the few words of arriving and departing crew members.

One person who had a dim view of the direction the marina was headed was Shelly Butler, captain of a Baywatch boat who had been piloting county lifeguard vessels stationed in the marina for more than thirty years. The boat on which we were given a tour of the marina and the three communities to the north from the perspective of the water had a Hollywood history. It was the original Baywatch boat—a small craft that lifeguards employed to save lives—used to film the first season of the world's most popular television series, which went by the same name.

Butler was a one-man chamber of commerce for the marina and lifeguards, but he slipped off script when we passed the *Princess*. "I'll say one thing about this marina," he remarked: "they are pushing out the little guy" with larger slips and higher fees. We were on our way toward Mother's Beach, a protected sandy cove deep within the still water of the marina that was perfect for children, except for the constant high levels of pollution recorded there. To Butler and others higher on the chain of command of county lifeguards, there is no such thing as pollution either at Mother's Beach or at any beach along the shoreline of Santa Monica Bay. Such an admission would reduce crowds and their budget. To make this point, Butler went into a series of fake spasms that mocked illnesses. "See, I'm alright. Okay?"

Although Butler didn't mention it, the county had installed a fan with two paddle-type propellers at a cost of nearly $1 million to dissipate the high bacterial concentrations at Mother's Beach. A smaller aerator hadn't worked, and it didn't seem that this one was doing the job either. At one time a "bird excluder monofilament line" had been stretched across the water to prevent small birds from dropping fecal matter. The line did not deter the birds.

As we sped north from the entrance to the marina on the twin diesel, thirty-two-foot Baywatch boat, Butler pointed out where riptides would form later in the day. It was his job, with accompanying lifeguards, and sometimes towing Jet Skis, to swoop into the surf, pluck distressed swimmers from the frothy water, and deposit them safely on the beach. Rips were responsible for 90 percent of the rescues. Three weeks earlier on a Friday, there had been thirty-nine

rescues on Venice beaches. Minor chores included towing disabled boats to the marina, dealing with medical emergencies, taking ill children on Baywatch Make-A-Wish Foundation trips, herding wayward whales from the marina or extracting them from offshore nets, picking up body parts from airliners that crashed off Los Angeles International Airport, and rescuing would-be suicides.

Butler told a story about a jumper. A twenty-three-year-old Marina del Rey woman hitched a ride to the end of Sunset Boulevard and leaped out of the car. She stripped in front of startled diners at a seafood restaurant, dove into the water, and swam through the surf. She kept going past the point where more normal swimmers would have been exhausted. She swam with strong, sure strokes. Helicopters, Baywatch boats, and lifeguards on paddleboards searched the inland waters that night, but couldn't find her. The next morning a Coast Guard helicopter searching five miles out to sea saw what resembled an inflatable manikin in a jellyfish roll, meaning a draped position. "She picked up her hand," said Butler, "and she very weakly waved. That's when the excitement began." The woman had been in the water for nine hours during the chilly fall months. She was treated for hypothermia and extreme muscle exhaustion. No one had expected her to be alive. Butler told the story with the admiration of one expert swimmer for another.

As he passed the lifeguard towers on shore, Butler leaned over the side of the speeding boat each time and made a circular motion with his arm, indicating a close affinity with the lifeguards on the beach. To be a Los Angeles County lifeguard is to belong to a paramilitary group of superior swimmers whose aquatic caste system dates back to 1908 and the Hawaiian-born *haole* George Freeth, admiringly described by Jack London, who was attempting to learn how to surf on Waikiki Beach, as "standing upright on his board, carelessly poised, a young god bronzed with sunburn."[10]

Freeth was the trailblazer for the Z-Boy surfers and lifeguards like Shelly Butler. In Hawaii, Freeth rescued surfing from the oblivion to which missionaries had consigned it. He introduced stand-up surfing to Southern California on an eight-foot-long, two-hundred-pound wood surfboard on waves off Venice Beach in 1908. Freeth's heavy surfboard resembled a primitive door. The tapered planks with a rounded leading edge were held together by bulky cross members. He was also captain of the U.S. Volunteer Lifesaving Corps of Venice. Freeth was responsible, according to the Los Angeles County lifeguard website, "for what many consider the greatest rescue in our history."[11] For more than two hours Freeth swam through a pounding surf and gale-force winds to rescue seven fishermen in three swamped boats, making repeated trips back and forth through the cold, hypothermia-inducing water. He was awarded the Congressional Gold Medal, the highest award given a civilian by Congress. Freeth died at the age of thirty-five in the global flu pandemic of 1919. To the lifeguards who followed him, he was a true waterman, meaning he was at harmony with the ocean and used its various elements to surf and rescue people with confidence and élan. A bronze bust of Freeth that sat atop a monument commemorating him in Redondo Beach was stolen shortly after our outing with Butler. The copper content of the bronze was commanding high prices.

To prove there was no pollution, Butler and his two crewmen searched the waters for dolphins off Will Rogers State Beach at the northern end of Santa Monica. Three adults and one young dolphin appeared and played in the bow wave of the Baywatch boat as it cruised along at a moderate speed. "When I started out life-guarding in 1964," said Butler, "we never saw a dolphin, never." Butler then pointed the boat south, and we raced the six miles back to Marina del Rey as the radio crackled with the message that either firecrackers or an AK-47 were being discharged onshore.

The land was of a clayey consistency, and, as far as the eye could reach, entirely bare of trees and even shrubs; and there was no sign of a town,—not even a house to be seen. What brought us into such a place, we could not conceive. No sooner had we come to anchor, than the slip-rope, and the other preparations for south-easters, were got ready; and there was reason enough for it, for we lay exposed to every wind that could blow, except the north-west, and that came over a flat country with a range of more than a league of water.
Richard Henry Dana Jr., 1835

THE INDUSTRIAL COAST

San Pedro Bay, a broad open roadstead lying eastward of Point Fermin, which formerly afforded good shelter only in northerly and westerly winds, has been converted by the Government into a safe harbor for all winds and swell by the construction of a breakwater which is now (1908) almost completed. . . . San Pedro, on the western shore of San Pedro Harbor, is the principal town, and is the seaport for Los Angeles, about 21 miles inland. The depths alongside the wharves range from 20 to 24 feet, according to locality. There is a large amount of domestic commerce in lumber, general merchandise, grain, fish, and dairy products, and the port has a rapidly increasing foreign commerce.
United States Coast Pilot, 1909

I live on a bluff overlooking Los Angeles Harbor and the ocean. From my window on a clear winter day I can see the snowcapped peak of Mount Baldy where I could be skiing. Below me is the line of breakers on the ocean side of Cabrillo Beach, populated by a few surfers, one or two hardy swimmers, and a few happy wanderers soaking in the aloneness of a winter beach.
Philip L. Fradkin, *California*, 1974

Traffic Separation Scheme, Los Angeles/Long Beach, also known as Traffic Separation Scheme, Gulf of Santa Catalina, is in the approaches to Los Angeles/Long Beach. . . . Traffic lanes have been designated to aid in the prevention of collisions at the approaches to major harbors along heavily traveled waters, but are not intended in any way to supersede or to alter the applicable Navigation Rules. **United States Coast Pilot, 2006** have been camped for three days at Jalama Beach County Park, halfway between Point Conception and Point Arguello. The fall weather has been beyond perfect, once again giving the lie to the reputation of Point Conception as the Cape Horn of the Pacific. I watched surfers thread their way between deadly rocks at the appropriately named Tarantulas, got the soles of my walking shoes clogged with tar from natural oil seeps, and watched the southerly arc of the launch of a rocket from nearby Vandenberg Air Force Base carrying an Italian satellite into space. Forty-four years earlier on another balmy night, I had passed offshore of this beach and the two points in a twenty-two-foot sailboat bound from San Francisco to Los Angeles and a new job. From my campground site, I saw the square bulk of a large container ship slowly edge its way toward Los Angeles Harbor.

The next day I was in the Los Angeles Pilot Station at the end of Signal Street in San Pedro tracking the progress of the *Hatsu Excel* on a large, high-definition computer screen. The *Excel,* one of the newer, large-capacity container vessels, was nearing the end of a ten-day voyage from Qingdao, a major seaport in China's Shandong Province. Its carrying capacity was rated at 6,332 containers having a length of twenty feet. The *Excel* was carrying forty-foot containers, thus halving its rated capacity on this trip. Considering the time of year, which was late October, and the type of cargo usually destined for Los Angeles from China, most of those containers were destined to satisfy the Christmas cravings of customers in big box stores such as Costco, Target, and Wal-Mart.

Few people are aware of how their goods are delivered to them, and consequently very little public attention is paid to the Port of Los Angeles. The port lies south of the zone where all the activities for which the city is famed, and most of its affluent residential areas, are located. Below Los Angeles International Airport, the South Bay social and economic curtain hides the Industrial City, unknown to almost all except its workers and inhabitants. Like the powerful engine hidden deep within the bowels of a ship, the port generates the movement of goods that flow through the city, the Southwest, and the nation.

The Port of Los Angeles branded itself "America's Port" in the new millennium, a more realistic assessment of its role than the "Worldport LA" brand employed near the end of the twentieth century. It ranks first in the nation in the number of containers handled and the total value of foreign trade, primarily with Asian nations. By itself Los Angeles ranks thirteenth in container volume in the world; but when combined with the adjacent Port of Long Beach, the two Southern California ports rank fifth. Where the trade was once in substantial items such as coal, lumber, and grain and other farm products, the imported goods now consist mainly of furniture, clothing, automobile parts, electronic products, and toys.

A huge infrastructure has been established to handle this massive trade. The mantra of the port is to grow through constant modernization in order to handle greater and greater amounts of cargo. A highly placed port official told me that his executive director was not happy unless she spent one million dollars a day, meaning large chunks of money over short periods of time. That money does not come from taxpayers, nor does it go to taxpayers. A former mayor attempted to tap the port's revenue, but failed in court. The money generated by the port goes to the port, originally formed to satisfy the city's trade and travel needs but now serving a far larger constituency.

The physical infrastructure of the port consists of twenty-seven terminals, 270 berths, and seventeen marinas on forty-three hundred acres of what once was marshland and open water but is now filled land. Sticking into the air or crawling along on the ground are giant hammerhead cranes, tank farms, long trains, and extensive lines of trucks. Not only do 8.3 million containers with cargo valued at $240.4 billion generating an annual operating revenue of $417.2 million pass through the port, but the harbor is also the major cruise ship terminal for the West Coast, handling 1.2 million passengers a year. These figures are for 2007, the last full year before the deep recession skewered them.[1]

The Port of Los Angeles—like the region itself—ranks number one in the nation in diversity of uses. Other than the expected industrial and accompanying port security facilities, there are two beaches—one badly polluted swimming beach inside the breakwater and a delightful ocean beach on the outside—a fishing pier, a bathhouse, a rental hall, an aquarium, a tiny wetland, a youth activities center, a boat-launching ramp, a hotel, four thousand pleasure boats and a few remaining commercial fishing vessels, restaurants and shops, a maritime museum, warehouses serving as film studios, a sewer treatment plant, a federal prison, a Coast Guard base, and a memorial to the small Japanese fishing community that vanished into detention camps at the start of World War II. The largest manmade harbor in the Western Hemisphere is enclosed by a nine-mile stone breakwater divided into thirds, with separate but equal entrances for the ports of Los Angeles and Long Beach.

The Spanish, who followed Cabrillo's 1542 voyage to Alta California on land more than two centuries later, had to choose between a partially protected ocean landing and freshwater twenty-two miles inland. Wisely, they chose to settle near the freshwater to the north. Los Angeles was a city that had to mold itself out of the raw materials of a desert and then remake itself repeatedly thereafter. It was not a ready-made city blessed with all the ingredients needed for a great metropolitan area, one of them being a natural harbor such as those at San Diego, San Francisco, and Seattle on the West Coast, Boston and New York City on the East Coast, and Savannah and New Orleans to the south. Los Angeles eventually imported freshwater from great distances to the north (Owens Valley and the Feather River) and the east (Colorado River), and walled off the salt water to the south in order to provide a sheltered harbor for ships. The modern harbor with its protective breakwater began life as mudflats and a tenuous anchorage one mile from the rocky beach and steep bluff. In time it bypassed its more organic competitors and became a huge artificial construct whose industrial fumes poisoned the region.

The *Hatsu Excel* plowed slowly toward what that once-primitive dent in the coast had become. The telegraph had replaced runners on horseback who used binoculars and telescopes to identify sailing vessels and then rode hard into San Pedro to alert the pilots and others. Satellites in space now do the same work. With global positioning satellites and an automatic identification system in the Vessel Tracking Center atop San Pedro Hill, the slow progress of the ship was monitored.

The giant container ship was headed due east in the western traffic lane at a speed of 8.7 knots, well below the required limit of 12 knots in the precautionary zone. The speed limit had been lowered as part of a broad program to reduce harmful fuel emissions. The Vessel Tracking Center began operation in 1994 after the 1989 Exxon *Valdez* oil spill in Alaska and a number of near misses and actual collisions on the approaches to the two Southern California ports.

The Los Angeles pilots are former tugboat or merchant ship captains who handle about five thousand vessel moves a year. They exude confidence. The chief pilot wears a cowboy hat. Other than an occasional Santa Ana wind from the north or the remnant of a hurricane from the south, the waters of San Pedro Bay and the interior channels are relatively calm, with only faint currents generated by moderate tides. The pilots advise ship captains, but most captains defer to the pilots and merely repeat their commands to the helmsmen.

Outside Angel's Gate, the opening in the breakwater leading to the Port of Los Angeles, there was a slight chop and dense fog. The captain of the pilot boat had the *Hatsu Excel* pinpointed on his radar screen three miles off the gate. "There she is," said the pilot. The silent vessel resembled a huge ghost ship slipping by in the opposite direction. The green markings of the Evergreen Shipping Agency, the

ship's name and its home port of London, were visible as the pilot boat circled around the stern and slowed to match the larger vessel's speed in the quiet water of its lee. A hop onto the swinging rope ladder with wooden steps, a thirty-foot climb to the sideport, and the pilot and his guest were aboard the moving ship.

The pilot was asked what he'd like to drink—coffee, please—and led quickly by a steward through a maze of corridors and stairs to the closed bridge that spread the width of the spotlessly clean ship. Its Japanese captain and crew wore identical khaki uniforms with no distinguishing insignias except the word *Evergreen* stitched over the left breast. The lone exception was the helmsman, who was clad in an orange jumpsuit and was steering the ship manually.

The pilot immediately took charge. "Everything in good order, Captain? Can we center this radar, Captain?" He asked if there was a lookout in the bow, beyond which nothing was visible from the bridge. The captain said there was. The ship was so large, the engines so quiet, and the fog so isolating that all sense of movement, other than the torpedo-shaped image of the container ship on the radar screen, was absent.

Pilot: "Steady."
Pilot: "Make it 330, please."
Captain: "330."
Helmsman: "330."

A few wisps of blue sky emerged above, the fog thinned, and the *Hatsu Excel* burst into the warm, bright sunshine of a fall day in Southern California. To port was the unmanned lighthouse. Behind the breakwater on the starboard side, two tugs waited for the pilot's command to move alongside. Then they nudged the vessel into the channel that crossed what remained of the bay stuffed almost to capacity by new terminals and guided it into the main channel leading to the Evergreen piers. At the pilot's command, the turn commenced in a basin that would line the vessel up with the pier, its bow pointed in the direction it would depart.

The breakwater *is* the harbor. The harbor *is* Los Angeles and, to a lesser extent, the nation. No breakwater, no harbor, and no Los Angeles in its present configuration and population, and no timely delivery of Christmas toys across the nation. Before any breakwaters were constructed, there were numerous wrecks when ships dragged their anchors in the partly sheltered roadstead during storms. Given a warning of approaching gales by telegraphed messages from San Francisco, captains raised their anchors and sought safety in the lee of Catalina Island. There were no warnings about storms and hurricanes approaching from the southeast, the most vulnerable direction for ships anchored in the bight of San Pedro Bay.

Asked at an 1896 congressional hearing to determine if a breakwater should be constructed at Santa Monica or San Pedro, a controversial issue that caused much debate at the time, a veteran pilot said the San Pedro location would be much safer. Since that was also the conclusion of three boards of inquiry, Congress agreed. The start of work on the breakwater in 1899 was celebrated by a free, two-day barbecue featuring six tons of beef. President William McKinley pushed a button in Washington, D.C., that sent the electric impulse to the machinery that

should have dumped the rocks in San Pedro, California. Nothing happened. The crowd of more than twenty thousand people waited, and the rocks finally had to be dumped by hand. The first stones came from a quarry on Catalina Island and the rest from two inland locations. The bottom of the breakwater is 48 feet wide and consists of rubble weighing between twenty pounds and one hundred tons pried by crowbar or dropped by derrick from railroad flatcars atop a parallel train trestle. The upper part of the breakwater extends 14 feet above low tide and is 20 feet wide at the top. The 11,080-foot-long San Pedro Breakwater ends at Angel's Gate Lighthouse. The distinctive lighthouse, often featured on literature promoting Los Angeles and its port, is of Romanesque design. It is easily the most unusual lighthouse on the West Coast, if not in the nation. It resembles a short, extended telescope standing on its lens. Automated now but manually operated when its light first shone in 1913, the ten-sided, three-story lighthouse is set on an octagonal base. Black columns divide the sides and are capped by a widow's walk. Battered by hurricanes, earthquakes, and a battleship, the lighthouse lists slightly. As if to emphasize its unique qualities, Angel's Gate is the only lighthouse on the West Coast to have a green, rather than a white, flashing light.

Construction of the first section of the outer breakwater was completed in 1912. The San Pedro Breakwater was a public works project as important to the future of Los Angeles as the construction of Hoover Dam, which would bring more electricity and water to the growing city. The commercial piers in Santa Monica, Redondo Beach, Long Beach, and elsewhere soon lost their commercial importance. A U.S. Army Corps of Engineers officer rhapsodized:

A vessel needs only to round the breakwater, even during severe storms and all is calm. There is no narrow, rock-lined channel to pass through, where any minute the ship may be ground to destruction, nor is there a seething breaking bar to cross, where water is scarce at best, and where the captain of a ship is in mortal terror that a swell may let his vessel onto the bottom and break her in two.[2]

Two additional segments of the breakwater, one called the Middle Breakwater and the other the Long Beach Breakwater, were built later. There were other important harbors enclosed by jetties at the time the San Pedro Breakwater was completed. They included Alexandria in Egypt, Cherbourg in France, Genoa in Italy, Plymouth in England, and Chicago, Buffalo, and Cleveland on the Great Lakes. Los Angeles would eventually surpass all of them in size and importance.

On the balmy day the *Hatsu Excel* passed through the gate, anglers sat on chairs atop the fitted boulders or poked for crabs in the breakwater's interstices at low tide. Years before, there had been a rusting, broken chain-link fence. Now there was an ineffective concrete barrier with threatening signs declaring no trespassing on the breakwater, to which no one paid attention. I had walked the nearly two miles to the lighthouse along this breakwater a number of times while living nearby for five years and had marveled at the seawall's resilience. Since the mid-1970s, however, the giant stones have been dislodged in a number of places, proving the breakwater, like the Santa Monica Pier, was not immune to the constant pounding of the ocean.

Walking on the breakwater once again, I could sense the energy from the waves breaking on the ocean side invisibly transmitted through the thick stone breakwater under my feet and generating smaller waves on the harbor side. Larger waves pounding the breakwater, and sometimes breaking over it, set up a bathtublike motion called a seiche in the harbor that makes it difficult for pilots to dock a vessel.

To Richard Henry Dana, the harbor serving El Pueblo de Los Angeles in prebreakwater years was not a happy place. In fact, he and other seamen referred to it as "the hell of California." Dana's ship had to anchor three miles offshore, which meant a long row. There was the fear of southwesters during the winter months and the constant need to remain alert. Hauling hides and supplies up and down the bluff was a backbreaking job. Two of the crew were flogged, unjustly by a cruel captain in Dana's estimation.

The names and histories of two islands within the bight indicated the raw materials from which the modern harbor would be shaped. A small, rocky islet that served as a cemetery in the midst of the bay came to symbolize for Dana the bleakness of the anchorage. An Englishman, who was the captain of a merchant vessel, was buried on the island. He was thought to have been poisoned by his first mate, said Dana, who was himself contemplating mutiny against his captain. "There it stood, desolate, and in the midst of desolation," wrote Dana, "and there were the remains of one who died and was buried alone and friendless."[3] At the nearby Battle of Dominguez Ranch during the Mexican-American War of 1846, between four and fourteen U.S. Marines were killed, the number varying according to the account. Their bodies were hauled to the bleak island and buried. The heap of rocks, fifty feet high and two acres of bare ground in extent, was labeled both Dead Man's and Deadman's Island on early charts. The holding ground surrounding it was designated "rocky."

Another island, technically a stretch of sand dunes forming a barrier island, was called Rattlesnake Island because of the snakes washed downstream and onto its shoreline during floods on the nearby Los Angeles and San Gabriel rivers. Deadman's and Rattlesnake islands were connected by a jetty in 1871, and the single channel underwent the first of many dredging operations. Gradually the sand dunes, interior breakwater, and Deadman's Island disappeared, the latter blasted into oblivion over a period of two years and its rocks and human bones scattered to fill what is now known as Reservation Point at the tip of Terminal Island.

The neatly trimmed trees and grass, and the white homes with roofs of Spanish tile at the end of the point, which have an unobstructed view of Angel's Gate, are an anomaly in the industrial landscape. They accommodate the commander of the Coast Guard base and warden of the adjacent Federal Correctional Institution that once housed such notables as Al Capone, Charles Manson, members of the Bonanno family celebrated in films and books about the Mafia, Timothy Leary of LSD fame, and G. Gor-

don Liddy of Watergate renown. The prison is known as "Club Fed" for its seaside setting and the less dangerous and generally more affluent criminals it houses. But the double fence, multiple rolls of concertina wire, and tall guard towers signify dangerous presences of some kind.

Rattlesnake Island has fattened beyond recognition over the years, has lost any similarity to a real island, and has become a series of ruler-straight shapes designed to receive, move, and transport containers in as efficient a manner as possible. Behind the federal presence to the north, and jutting beyond it in a fishhook shape on the remade island, are the newest terminals, numbered 300 and 400. There is a Fish Harbor, but there are no more canneries, whose pungent odors used to waft over the town. As at Monterey, more fish were landed at Terminal Island for a period of time than anywhere else in the country. The tuna disappeared, the canneries moved overseas, and cans of tuna fish are now shipped to Los Angeles in containers from foreign countries. There were also shipyards on Terminal Island and elsewhere within the port with names like Todd, Bethlehem, and Cal Ship that employed more than ninety thousand workers at the peak of their production during World War II. They, too, have moved elsewhere.

The Port of Los Angeles has become a container monoculture serving a consumption-hungry public, a fact most evident on Terminal Island. Burly longshoremen lugging cargo on their shoulders and backs, and cranes on ships lifting pallets of goods, preceded container ships. The *Hawaiian Merchant* was the first container vessel to call at the port. Two years later in 1960, the Matson Navigation Company became the first shipping firm to lease container space. The port handled seven thousand containers that year. Matson's high-volume Pacific Coast–Hawaiian freight service, along with jet aircraft, soon displaced its more traditional passenger service.

Cranes were still prevalent in the 1970s, but shipping was moving rapidly toward standardization and speed, which meant containers of the same size that could be loaded, unloaded, and loaded again and again on ships, trucks, trains, and planes. *Intermodal* and *multimodal* became transportation buzzwords. Container traffic grew from 633,000 units in 1980 to 2.1 million in 1990, the second year Los Angeles led the nation; to 4.9 million in 2000, the port's sixth year as leader; and to 8.3 million in 2007, its eighth consecutive year leading the nation.

Why the container companies are located on the greatly expanded Terminal Island is evident from the history of Kaiser Point and Berth 46 on the west side of the main channel. The industrial development of the nascent port began adjacent to the business and residential sections of San Pedro. The port and community have engaged in a pas de deux over the years. The mutually dependent partners have danced to different tempos: San Pedro slowly and languorously, the port fast and furiously. The transfer of dangerous cargoes gradually shifted inland to the Wilmington area and eastward to the northern end of Terminal Island, for good reasons.

There were a number of marine disasters in the outer harbor that rocked the community. The *Ada Hancock,* which shuttled passengers and freight from anchored ships to a San Pedro pier, blew up under mysterious circumstances off Deadman's Island in 1863. Twenty-six people were killed and a large shipment of Wells Fargo gold, the attempted theft of which may have been the cause of the explosion, sank to the bottom of the bay. Explosives were stored on board the *Hancock,* and shots were heard before the blast. Phineas Banning, the first developer of the harbor area, was blown clear of the vessel. His chief clerk and brother-in-law were killed, and his wife and mother were injured, along with many others. Banning found himself dazed on a sandbar. He lived to build a three-story mansion in the Greek Revival style in Wilmington the next year and to prosper from his maritime investments.

Toluene, a highly volatile petroleum product used in the production of TNT, leaked from the tanker *Fredricksburg* operated by the War Shipping Administration during World War II. It began drifting with the tidal current from Berth 151 across the Turning Basin to Berth 223 shortly after midnight on October 21, 1944. Someone smelled gasoline fumes, the Coast Guard investigated, determined their source, but did nothing. The next afternoon a welder working on a navy vessel at Berth 223 set off a flash fire that immediately engulfed the navy ships under construction, parked vehicles, and the surrounding piers. Thirty-two people were killed and more than thirty-five were hospitalized, some with severe burns.

Two years after World War II ended, the tanker *Markay* was taking on a load of gasoline to be delivered to the San Francisco Bay Area when there was a violent explosion followed by others at the Shell Oil Company pier in the Wilmington Harbor area. Sheared rivets fell as far as five miles away in San

Pedro, a portion of the deck was blown eight hundred feet into the offices of the Texaco Oil Company, the tanker broke in two, and the fire spread quickly from Berth 167 across the channel to the American President Lines piers. Six ships were towed to safety, and the fire threatened fuel storage tanks for ten hours. Eleven people were killed and twenty-three injured.

Shortly after a liquefied natural gas terminal—harboring its own particular set of dangers—had been approved by the port commission, a Union Oil Company supertanker exploded on December 17, 1976, at Berth 46 in the outer harbor, the location for the proposed natural gas facility. Berth 46 was close to San Pedro residences. The force of the explosion broke windows in a wide area and was heard forty miles distant. The 810-foot *Sansinina* was blown into three separate parts. Two pieces assumed the wide V-shape of a tilted bow and stern. The midsection was blown onto the wharf, which caught fire. It took four days to extinguish the blaze. One port security guard and eight crewmen were killed. Other crewmen, who had been eating in the stern section, were blown clear and survived with various injuries.

Up to this time the community of San Pedro had been fairly passive. The *Sansinina* disaster jolted residents into action. They vigorously opposed the natural gas terminal to no avail. The terminal was approved by the Los Angeles City Council, but was not built, for safety and economic reasons determined by others outside the vortex of city politics. The port then began developing plans to move liquefied bulk transfer facilities and storage tanks holding oil and toxic products from populated areas to sections of

Terminal Island to be created by dredging channels to accommodate deeper-draft vessels. The bay would be filled with the spoils. Along the way, those plans changed when more lucrative leases with container companies became a possibility. In this manner, Terminals 300 and 400, the single largest expansion program in the port's history and perhaps in the history of any U.S. port, became realities in the late 1990s and early 2000s, when the container trade boomed.

In order to expand, however, the ports of Los Angeles and Long Beach were required by the California Coastal Commission to finance a similar, or in-kind, mitigation. Los Angeles sank $55 million into restoring Batiquitos Lagoon in northern San Diego County. Los Angeles and the Port of Long Beach together spent $102 million purchasing and restoring 590 acres of the 1,200-acre Bolsa Chica Wetlands in Orange County. Shallow water habitats for birds and fishes were constructed in San Pedro Bay, and a 3.2-acre wetland was created near the marine aquarium at Cabrillo Beach. The tiny wetland was all that remained of the 3,450 acres of marshlands that once ringed the bay. Considering the revenue the two terminals would generate, the many millions of dollars spent on mitigation were a bargain.

Besides the *Sansinina* disaster, there were two other events that would dramatically alter the direction of the port's development and force its semiautonomous governing body to comply with outside forces. In 1998, the California Air Resources Board identified particulate matter in diesel exhausts, more commonly known as soot, as a toxic air contaminant. Diesel exhaust is a complex mixture of poisonous chemicals, many of which have not yet been identified. The emissions from diesel engines cause most of the cancers attributable to air pollution in California. Besides lung cancer, the sooty carbon particles cause asthma, difficulty in breathing, and other health problems. They also add to global warming. The two ports are the greatest contributors to this toxic mess, thus making them the single largest source of air pollution in the region of greatest air quality degradation in the country.

The closer to the source, the greater the threat to health. A study of air pollution in U.S. ports stated with reference to Los Angeles and Long Beach: "The combination of growing port activity, the densely populated region, and a wind pattern that accumulates rather than disperses air pollution from port activities creates a 'perfect storm' of threats to public health."[4] Ships under way or docked and generating electricity, tugboats, yard equipment at terminals, the thousands of moving and idling trucks that pass through the harbor area daily, the diesel-driven trains that transport containers, and other mechanized equipment produce the lethal brew. An air pollution forum sponsored by the Los Angeles city councilwoman who represented the San Pedro area was titled "Do You Live in a Diesel Death Zone?" Posing the question in such a manner suggested that residents did, indeed, live in just such a place.

In order to meet federal and state air quality requirements, the two ports adopted a Clean Air Action Plan in 2006. The slow speed of the *Hatsu Excel* on its approach to the harbor, which lessened emissions, was part of that plan. Lower sulfur levels in fuel was

another. Ships burn the dirtiest of all fuels in the largest of all engines. Parts of the plan have either been implemented or challenged. Truckers were one of the first affected groups to go to court. Truck traffic is huge: eight million movements through the ports in a year, sixteen thousand through the Port of Los Angeles in a day. The 16,800 older and dirtier trucks that regularly deliver or pick up containers in the ports contribute the most smog: an amount that exceeds what the six million cars in the region produce. The Port of Los Angeles has also dragged its feet, not wanting to impose air quality requirements on expansion plans that might put it at a competitive disadvantage with other ports.

There was a second challenge to the aloofness of the Port of Los Angeles from its immediate surroundings. Neighborhood groups, some cognizant of the *Sansinina* disaster, didn't like the plans for the development of the 174-acre China Shipping Terminal in the inner harbor. The terminal was being built by the port for the China Shipping Group, a state-owned conglomerate. Local residents were joined by the Natural Resources Defense Council and other environmental groups who filed suit in 2001 citing the lack of a proper environmental impact statement. The megaterminal was already under construction near residences and schools. The State Court of Appeals halted all work on the first phase of construction, which was 90 percent complete, pending a full environmental review that would take years to complete and delay other port expansion projects. The court's action and its implications sent a chill through all ports in the country.

The Port of Los Angeles settled the suit in 2003,

agreeing to much that would later be incorporated into the air quality plan. Part of the settlement called for a $50 million fund to mitigate impacts on the surrounding community, including $10 million for cleaner trucks and $20 million for parks and landscaping in San Pedro and Wilmington. The port could now proceed with its plans to expand cruise ship traffic in the harbor where the television series *The Love Boat* had been filmed.

Ports are big businesses, and like any business they have competitors. Gulf and East Coast ports seek to take business from West Coast ports and vice versa. Ports are also economic indicators, and some investors watch them for clues about which way the economy is moving. On the international level, the full containers that arrive and the empties that are returned to Asia from Los Angeles are visible indications of the lack of balance of trade. When I visited the port in the fall of 2008, at a time when the national economy was in free fall, shipping was down considerably from the previous year. What was particularly eerie, and *eerie* was the precise word used by a port official, was that there was only a slight peak in Christmas season traffic during the summer and early fall months, a reflection of the expectations of American retailers. The *Hatsu Excel* was delivering one of the last loads of such goods in late October. It would move on again within forty-eight hours for Oakland, then to various Chinese ports, before returning to Los Angeles in one month.

The terminal where the ship docked, known as "Evergreen Los Angeles" on computer-generated order forms, is the fulcrum in getting manufactured items, say a pair of cross-training shoes, from the factory in China to the outlet store in Des Moines. The port is where the means of transportation switches from waterborne to land-based.

Work began on simultaneously unloading and loading the *Hatsu Excel* the next morning with the help of information that zipped back and forth over computers from Asia to North America, and plans drawn up on the second floor of the Evergreen terminal building. The Taiwan-based Evergreen Marine Corporation is one of the port's oldest container companies, having established its first container operation in North America in 1976 on Terminal Island. It is among the largest such corporations in the world, serving more than eighty countries. The Evergreen facility occupies 205 acres on Terminal Island and has a capacity of 31,200 twenty-foot containers or their equivalents.

The land-based operations of all container shipping companies have certain similarities. Costs are paramount. Standardization and speed of movement are givens. All movements are carefully planned and implemented in control rooms thick with computers, their screens displaying the various locations of containers and the movements of machinery, and with various types of communication equipment. There is a gang boss for each ship who has the necessary paperwork generated by the planners. There are controllers in the terminal building and a gang in the yard for each piece of moving equipment. Complex movements mesh, most of the time. Sometimes there are equipment failures and accidents resulting in injuries or deaths and delays. When the system breaks down and becomes clogged, a "trouble condition" exists.

69

There is a push to get the cargo off and on the ships as fast as possible. It begins with a charge of people resembling medieval yeomen storming the steel walls of a castle. Armored in colorful safety vests, longshoremen and -women called lashers rush the steel gangway with twenty-four-foot aluminum poles resembling pikes to loosen the lashings that hold containers in place. When the mechanized equipment moves into action, so does the equipment positioning system. There are hand signals, radio communications, computer and television screens, and global positioning satellites to help determine exact movements.

Directions to each gang, or to the operator of a yard vehicle in the Evergreen terminal, come from a controller at one of ten work stations, who has a clear view of the yard plus two computer screens. One screen has cues, meaning a list of tasks. The other has a map of the yard. Purple rectangles mean stacked containers; green rectangles portray containers sitting on a chassis. Trucks and yard vehicles move around, leaving snail trails on computer screens behind them.

This day two container ships are being simultaneously unloaded and loaded at the Evergreen facility, which has two post-Panamax berths and eight post-Panamax gantry cranes, or hammerheads, as they are also called. (*Post-Panamax* refers to vessels too large for the Panama Canal.) There are seventy management employees. Depending on the daily workload, the longshoremen and -women can range from forty to the hundreds. Today the number is close to the higher limit. They don't work regular hours but are on call.

The scene, to a stranger, is one of controlled chaos. The controllers bark into their handheld radios:

"Send it back. I have to have that tophandler take it off. Do you copy, Ray? Okay Ray, stop what you are doing. Ray, go off and load that other can."

"Turns his radio off, that son of a bitch."

The controller in the neighboring cubicle laughs at his colleague's problems. "Frank, tell him to read his screen, for Christ's sake. Oh, look at this. The guy's not reading his screen. It ain't working."

Somehow, it does work—most of the time.

Outside, the trucks entering the yard have to clear three gates. At the first gate, a combination of human inspection and electronic scanning devices determines the driver's, the truck's, and the container's identification, and ascertains, for security purposes, that there is only one person in the cab. Safety equipment and compliance with air quality standards are checked at the second. At the third gate, there is a security check, and a gate pass and mission slip are issued if all is okay. If not, then the driver parks and walks to the "trouble window" for manual processing.

On a busy day, trucks are waiting at the various gates like horses stacked up for a series of races. Diesel fumes thicken the air. Evergreen and other terminals are moving toward automation, such as optical character recognition systems, to hasten the process. There are between nineteen hundred and twenty-one hundred truck moves on a busy day at Evergreen. Twenty-eight minutes is the average time between a truck's entry into and departure from the facility.

The tall hammerhead cranes that visibly define a

port hold operators who peer downward and manipulate joysticks that clamp a twelve-ton spreader with four pins into square four-inch holes on top of the four corners of a container, twist the pins to lock them in place, lift the container upward, and then drop it with a slight thud onto various types of flat chassis pulled by truck cabs lined up alongside the *Hatsu Excel*. Thirty containers can be moved by the gantry cranes in an hour, meaning an average of one every two minutes. "Everything in this industry is about time," a woman crane operator told me.

The operators have no idea what they are lifting. The cabs are air conditioned, the seats comfortable. Because of the strain on backs bent over for long periods of time to view the loads, a full shift consists of four hours. Back injuries are common. Smaller staple-shaped cranes on rubber wheels, called transtainers, are remotely guided along rows by GPS signals. Utility tractors move cargo along and between rows. Depending on where the containers are located in a stack, side picks or top handlers are employed. For safety reasons, four loaded and five empty containers constitute a stack. White containers with green trim are refrigerated. They are called "reefers."

In addition to trucks, diesel-powered freight trains with fifty-six double-stacked flatcars transport loads north along the Alameda Corridor. Evergreen has four working tracks on the far side of the Vincent Thomas Bridge from the two berths. Almost four times as many containers are moved by trucks as by trains. The Alameda Corridor is the freeway equivalent for freight trains, linking the two ports with the East Los Angeles rail hub. For half of its twenty-mile length, the fifty-foot-wide corridor with three parallel train tracks lies within a trench. The $2.4 billion project eliminated more than two hundred dangerous railroad crossings and delays for both train and vehicular traffic. About eighteen thousand trains pass through the corridor in a year at speeds up to forty miles per hour. An expressway for trucks parallels the train corridor.

The harbor's influence flows eastward, where there are huge truck and train yards and warehouses near San Bernardino. There, in what is called the Inland Empire, the merchandise is sorted, repacked, stored, and sent on its way again to Dallas, Chicago, Atlanta, and New York City. Plans exist to push the corridor past the mountains and into the deserts of San Bernardino and Riverside counties, thus giving the port a grip upon the desert landscape extending from offshore waters. The map depicting the Alameda Corridor–East Project has a broad arrow pointing eastward. It's labeled "Trade Corridor to America." But consistency in the movement of freight, as has been demonstrated, is not a given. The widening of the Panama Canal, due to be completed in 2014, could shift the delivery of Asian goods to southern and eastern ports. Meanwhile, Mexico and Canada are poised to welcome shipping if the Port of Los Angeles falters.

Suffice it to say that San Diego is a prosperous, energetic place, which is rapidly adding to its present population of some forty thousand contented people. . . . Three schooners lay at the wharves, and two large lumber schooners swung in the tideway. A knot of torpedo boats were anchored on the Coronado side of the bay. . . . In the south, beyond the forlorn wastes of National City, rose wistful and pale the blue highlands of Mexico. **J. Smeaton Chase, 1910**

THE MILITARY COAST

For landing and taking on board hides, San Diego is decidedly the best place in California. The harbor is small and land-locked; there is no surf; the vessels lie within a cable's length of the beach; and the beach itself is smooth, hard sand, without rocks or stones.
Richard Henry Dana Jr., 1835

The harbor is being improved by the government with a view of obtaining a depth of 28 feet in the channel across the bar. . . . The bar rarely breaks, due to the protection of the thick kelp bed extending southward and westward from Point Loma. In 1908 this kelp was much thinner than usual. *United States Coast Pilot*, **1909**

Depressions have touched lightly on San Diego. Establishment of Army and Navy bases during the World War, completion of the San Diego and Arizona Eastern Railway in 1919, and the expositions of 1915–16 and 1935–36 have contributed to its prosperity. The outdoors, however, is San Diego's chief commodity, and tourists are its best customers. *The WPA Guide to California*, **1939**

The boundary between the United States and Mexico is marked by a 14-foot white marble obelisk on a pedestal 41 feet above the water near the edge of a low table bluff. The visible marker is 200 yards from the beach and 10 miles 142 degrees from Point Loma Light. A large circular concrete arena is conspicuous just S of the marker. *United States Coast Pilot*, **2006**

Without a harbor, San Diego would be just a very pleasant beach city near the Mexican border. "America's Finest City," as San Diego calls itself, can thank the accidents of geology and geography and its own perspicacity for its booming growth. The Rose Canyon Fault that progressively tore open the desert landscape of San Diego over tens of thousands of years in a north-south direction was the geological accident. The geographical accident was the proximity of the Pacific Ocean, whose waters flooded the fault zone and formed San Diego Bay. With the creation of the Silver Strand from the northward flow of sand disgorged from the Tijuana River along the Coronado shoreline, a harbor was formed.

The story of the navy in this company town is very much the tale of San Diego Bay, where sailors from one nation or another have been a constant and dominant presence for nearly five hundred years. The first known Europeans to land upon what would become known as California in 1542 sought refuge from winds and waves in this sheltered harbor, as do the modern warships of the U.S. Navy.

In recent years many military bases have closed along the coast, but not in San Diego, which is trying desperately to promote the fact that the city is something else—like a safe tourist haven or a high-tech research center—rather than the dominant fortress it remains. For years California led the nation in defense spending, and San Diego led California. The urban historian Roger W. Lotchin wrote in *Fortress California*: "California cities have pioneered in the domestication of the art of war, and San Diego has led the way in California, using essentially military resources to make itself into a great American urban center. More than any other Golden State city, the Port of the Palms has linked its fate to that of military development. It has been and is the quintessential martial metropolis."[1]

The money spent in San Diego County for military purposes, meaning for the navy and marines, tops that of any other county in the nation. Nearly three hundred thousand people are employed either directly or indirectly by the military in the region, a number that accounts for 20 percent of total employment, or one in five individuals, most of them centered in or from cities immediately circling San Diego. The full impact of the military presence accounts for a gross regional product of $18.3 billion in 2004 dollars. Since 9/11, defense spending has surged nearly 25 percent; and with the looming economic and military might of China and more of the U.S. fleet being deployed to the West Coast, that amount is expected to continue rising.

Underneath the theme park surfaces of San Diego lies a discordant city not mentioned in guidebooks or promotional literature. It consists of foul ocean and bay waters, a shallow bay that needs constant dredging, disappearing beaches, and the return of the Spanish speakers. San Diego has depended on the largess of the federal government to supplement the shortcomings of geology and geography and to erect barriers to keep out aliens.

Juan Rodríguez Cabrillo, possibly of Spanish descent, led the first European expedition to what is now the coast of California in 1542. He was a wanderer and an adventurer who was accompanied by three ships and approximately two hundred and fifty men whose goals were to settle the coast and search for the Spice Islands, meaning China, to the west. On September 28 the expedition discovered "a sheltered port and a very good one" at that.[2] The Spanish conversed haltingly with a few Kumeyaay Indians; noticed dense palls of smoke inland (as they would later at San Pedro) that hinted at a large native population; waited out a storm inside San Diego Bay; and then departed after five days for Catalina Island and points further north, claiming all the land along the coast for the king of Spain and the viceroy of Mexico.

Cabrillo touched a number of places mentioned in this book. He and his men rounded Point Conception and noticed the change in the weather as they continued to tack north into chilly waters against the strengthening and prevailing northwest winds. Searching for a great river whose origins were supposedly deep within the continent, but which was later proved to be a myth, the expedition missed the entrance to San Francisco Bay but sighted Point Reyes, which they named Cabo de Pinos for the dense groves of pines and firs on the ridges. From this point the expedition returned south, passing by Monterey Bay and the snowcapped mountains along the Big Sur coast and eventually arriving at Catalina, where they wintered. Cabrillo broke a limb—a leg, an arm, or both—which led to his death on January 3, 1543. The expedition was a failure, having met none of its objectives.

Other than a few momentary interruptions by Europeans, the Kumeyaay retained the desert coast for themselves after Cabrillo's departure. Then in 1769, things changed, radically. With the Russians

threatening from the north, the Spanish decided to permanently settle Southern California, then known as Alta California. Two ships, with their crews decimated by scurvy, reached San Diego first. They were followed on land by an advance party and then Father Junípero Serra bearing the cross and Gaspar de Portolá with the necessary armaments. Serra and Portolá arrived on July 1, 1769, the day it might be said that California was officially settled by Europeans and San Diego "first recognized the importance of war to the city-building process."[3] Serra said mass, and the ships' guns roared a salute.

To the expedition's diarist, San Diego was a "pleasant port." He added: "The beach abounds in large sardines, star fish, other species of fish, and mussels. All these heathen are fishermen, and they go to sea in rafts made of tule. The country consists of high hills, all of earth and without stones, and all covered with green grass and good pasture for every kind of stock."[4] Alta California changed hands, from Spain to Mexico, in 1821. It was during the Mexican occupation that the shallowness of the bay was first noticed. Richard Henry Dana described the torturous entrance to the harbor in 1835: "The entrance is so narrow as to admit but one vessel at a time, the current swift, and the channel runs so near to a low stony point that the ship's sides appeared almost to touch it."[5] The point was Ballast Point, behind which most sailing vessels anchored and nuclear submarines are now docked.

Compared to other ports and anchorages along the coast where Dana loaded and unloaded hides, San Diego was, he thought, by far the best for that particular purpose. The water was calm, the shore sandy and low, and gray whales cavorted in the shallow bay waters, where they gave birth to their young. A rotting presidio overlooked a collection of huts. On departing, Dana's vessel engaged in a race with another sailing ship but went aground and had to return and wait for high tide, the tidal level to which nuclear aircraft carriers are restricted when arriving or departing.

Dana and others thought the naval future of California lay in deeper and larger San Francisco Bay, but they didn't factor in the effectiveness of San Diego's dedicated lobbying and the San Francisco Bay Area's lack of unified interest in a military presence, which eventually resulted in the loss of major naval bases at Mare Island, Treasure Island, Hunters Point, Alameda, and Moffett Field. Altogether the Bay Area took the largest base-closing hit in the country during the 1990s, while San Diego emerged relatively unscathed.

Ten years after Dana's departure, the capture of San Diego during the war with Mexico and the hoisting of the American flag for the first of many tens of thousands of times in this flag-conscious military town was something less than thrilling. The *Cayne,* a twenty-two-gun sloop, rounded Point Loma after a three-day run from Monterey, crossed the bar with less than one foot to spare, and anchored in light winds on July 29, 1846. Next day the Marines landed near what is now the Marine Corps Recruit Depot, "took possession" of the settlement that is now Old Town, and hoisted the flag as a handful of dumbstruck inhabitants looked on. Over the next two days the seasick volunteers who constituted the ragtag battalion commanded by Major John C. Frémont came ashore at the mouth of False Bay, where the San

Diego River emptied into San Diego Bay. False Bay is now the artificially contrived Mission Bay, and the San Diego River now runs to the ocean between two concrete banks to the north.

For a little more than sixty years, San Diego slumbered with no serious purpose other than to remain placid and pleasant. It was a distant appendage to thriving Los Angeles to the north. Then in 1908 it found its true mate, pursued it vigorously, and hasn't let go of the navy since then. The navy returned the fervor of the embrace. It can be said that no large American city—San Diego being the sixth largest in the nation—has been and remains so locked in step with the military over such a long period of time, during which the two have mutually enriched each other.

The bay and an adequate port were the means of growth for San Diego, and by the 1890s it was obvious that large navy and commercial ships could not enter the shallow harbor. So San Diego businessmen within the Chamber of Commerce hit upon the policy of enticing the navy to San Diego in order to deepen the harbor at someone else's expense. At first the navy preferred San Francisco for a West Coast coaling station, but local pressure in the form of lavish entertainments prevailed in 1904. The first dredging followed three years after San Diego got its first shoreline-based navy facility.

When President Theodore Roosevelt dispatched the Great White Fleet to San Francisco in 1908, and then commanded it to circle the globe, San Diego was not a designated port of call. Under the aegis of the chamber, which was to emerge as, and remains, a very effective civic lobbying arm (and a power unto itself) for the navy's continuing presence, a small vessel was chartered. It steamed south to the western shore of Baja California to intercept the fleet and plead with its commanding admiral for the honor of being the first West Coast port to welcome the mighty armada of warships. The admiral agreed, decreeing that the destroyers would enter the bay, but that the battleships would remain anchored off the Silver Strand because of their deep draft and the shallowness of the bay.

The celebration, lasting for four days and nights, was immense. Thirty-three thousand oranges were delivered to the ships, along with armfuls of flowers carried by beauteous San Diego women. The ships' searchlights played at night over the sky and water off the Hotel del Coronado, masts were festooned with lights, staccato signals flashed back and forth between ships, and great bonfires blazed on shore. Downtown San Diego was a constant carnival and parade. Dances were held in hotels, and bars and brothels were filled to overcrowding. The navy quickly recognized that it was dearly loved in this city.

The first dredging of the harbor at federal expense was undertaken in 1907, but by the time the fleet arrived the depth over the bar at the entrance, and the sharp turn at Ballast Point, had shoaled. In 1910 the cruiser *California,* drawing twenty-seven feet, gingerly entered the harbor and anchored in midchannel, where, until later in the century, larger vessels had to remain. For the next one hundred years the federal government continually dredged the harbor as the draft of ships increased and additional facilities were needed onshore. Growth here, as it did

in San Pedro Bay, led to landfills that became a complex of separate bases, civilian facilities such as the airport, and the entire central and northern shoreline of the bay as it is known today.

There were other benefits in the partnership. To accommodate the growth it caused during World War II, the navy financed the water system that brought Colorado River water to San Diego. Retired officers went to work for local governments and businesses. The largest number of military retirees in the nation settled in the San Diego region, where post exchanges and military hospitals lessened the cost of living and defense-oriented contractors and research laboratories welcomed them as employees. It didn't hurt that the weather was balmy and the natives were friendly.

Sporadically at first before World War I, North Island, across the bay from the city and adjacent to Coronado, grew from a base for biplanes and amphibians into the center for naval aviation and the repository for more than one hundred nuclear bombs. In bits and pieces in a semicircle around the bay and stretching into outlying areas, other naval components were added over the years: a major hospital in Balboa Park and then another nearby to replace it, a marine base and naval training center near Lindbergh Field, shipyards and docks at Thirty-second Street, amphibious and submarine and destroyer and aircraft carrier bases that served as home ports for all but deep-draft battleships (declared obsolete while savvy San Diego concentrated on carriers), all types of secret electronic equipment bristling atop Point Loma and near Imperial Beach, the training of SEALs and sea mammals, other air bases at Miramar and Imperial Beach, secret test ranges on offshore

San Clemente Island, and research laboratories whose true purposes were hidden behind acronyms which, even if decoded, would still give no clue to their shifting missions.

As the favored navy tide advanced inexorably, the army retreated from its small footholds on Point Loma, North Island, and Imperial Beach. Why did San Diego mate so ardently and enduringly with the navy? Because the most patrician of all the military services offered a relatively clean engine of growth, enabling San Diego to remain the city beautiful it envisioned itself as being and, at the same time, to grow seamlessly into a martial metropolis.

Two San Diegans of differing perspectives have commented on this dependency. Bruce Linder, an author, defense consultant, and former navy captain wrote, referring to a local congressman: "Once a broad citywide consensus was reached, it continued unabated for decades to come. [Congressman William] Kettner's mastery of what years later would be called 'pork-barrel politics' had primed the pump of federal resources that would guarantee the uninterrupted flow of federal largess even to the present day. No city in America focused as single-mindedly on the Navy as did San Diego nor became as dependent on the vagaries of the federal government to augment its local economy."[6] Mike Davis, author, left-leaning social commentator, and University of California history professor, wrote that the militarization of San Diego's economy was "the epochal event in its twentieth-century history." He added in a cautionary tone: "Certainly San Diego elites have had to pay deference to the commanding role of the Pacific Fleet in the regional economy, stoking a repressive culture of superpatriotism and opening the inner sanctums of power to retired naval and marine brass." Since 1970, Davis noted, developers, landowners, and the navy "have deftly navigated around the bump in the road represented by San Diego's various environmental movements."[7]

San Diego exudes the impression of being a squeaky-clean, all-American city. Well, its bay and ocean waters are not clean, and herein lies a situation found elsewhere along the fabled Southern California coast. The navy gave and it took away. It gave sand to construct a modern city and replenish beaches, and it diminished the pristine quality of the waters by introducing aircraft carriers.

With naval aviation being pioneered and developed on North Island, various aircraft manufacturers scattered around the bay, and naval ships anchored or docked in the water, it was only a matter of time before aircraft carriers made San Diego their home port. The carriers were the greatest economic prize, more desired than even battleships because they were the biggest of all floating vessels; carried the largest number of personnel, who had the greatest number of dependents; and had the need for the most services. "The aircraft carrier," wrote Linder, "boldly propelled San Diego to the highest tier of American naval bases."[8]

The navy's first aircraft carrier entered San Diego Bay in November of 1924. The ungainly *Langly* was all flight deck superimposed over the traditional superstructure of a cruiser. With additional dredging in 1931, a member of the next generation of carriers, the *Saratoga*, balked by fog the first day, managed to navigate the twisting channel at high tide the next day. Although the *Saratoga* and another carrier were technically based just to the north, Los Angeles and Long Beach had other interests. Ever-aggressive San Diego eventually lured the two big ships southward.

With World War II looming, the navy, defense contractors, the Chamber of Commerce, civic leaders, and the media issued one of their periodic calls to arms, meaning more dredging that would simultaneously aid the national defense and the civilian maritime industry, the latter being of little consequence in San Diego. While costing only $1 million, land worth $3 million would be created, it was successfully argued. For the navy, this meant docking facilities for three new aircraft carriers.

The new nuclear carriers were a goal of the Chamber of Commerce's Military Affairs Department, whose acronym was MAD, from 1957 onwards. The first dredging appropriation for the carriers was made by Congress in 1960 and was followed by others. The same arguments and types of economic benefits, only this time amounting to $2.5 billion annually, were advanced in the mid-1990s, when the newest imperative was the creation of still deeper docking space, a turning basin, and an approach channel for three of the navy's newest nuclear carriers. San Diego, it was argued, had to beat out Long Beach, which was facing the loss of its naval shipyard and also vying for the carriers. The three new vessels would replace the two older steam-driven carriers that were no longer needed, at least in San Diego. Clean sand from the dredging would be dumped in the ocean off the depleted beaches of Oceanside, Del Mar, and Imperial Beach, where, it was assumed, it would spread shoreward—not a given, considering the erratic behavior of currents and sand. A coalition of beach cities favored having the sand pumped directly on nine beaches, a more costly process for the navy.

Beach replenishment—viewed as a God-given, or rather a navy-gifted, right in San Diego—is a bit of a misnomer. To replenish means to make complete again. The beaches had been historically narrow, the Silver Strand being a thin barrier spit when the Hotel Del was first built. They bulked up only when wide beaches were seen as a profitable tourist attraction, chambers of commerce promoted their mythic existence, and the navy supplied the sand—a massive thirty-seven million cubic yards to the Silver Strand since 1940, making it the most modified beach in California. There was a second purpose for the so-called replenishment. The sand was meant not only to give pleasure but also to protect coastal developments, which in San Diego County had been "built too low, too close to the beach, or without sufficient setbacks from cliff edges."[9]

Then, there was the matter of dirty sand. The contaminated spoils dredged from the turning basin adjacent to North Island that contained PCBs, heavy metals, and mercury from years of navy activities would be placed in a landfill and capped. This drew the attention of a nascent opposition, a new phenomenon in San Diego when it came to the navy and the harbor. A group of environmental, peace, antinuclear, and like-minded organizations filed suit alleging that all types of environmental and nuclear safety issues had not been addressed by the navy. The suit went nowhere, but it indicated that San

Diego was no longer a monolithic company town. "Thus environmental safety issues appear to have challenged the old booster consensus," wrote a local historian, "as no one and nothing had ever done in the past."[10]

The navy began dredging, with the clean sand going to replenish the nine beaches stretching from Oceanside to Imperial Beach. Problems developed. An unexploded mortar shell was found on the Oceanside beach where some of the sand had been pumped ashore. Dredging halted, then resumed with a screen placed over the vacuum to prevent sucking up more munitions. More ammunition was found. The sand was then dumped at sea, and the replenishment project was abandoned. There were more lawsuits.

The navy eventually got its deep water and the city its three carriers, each of which carries a crew totaling more than five thousand sailors and airmen, many of whom have onshore families. In sports-minded San Diego, where professional baseball and football teams have received substantial economic inducements from the city, a local official said: "Carrier homeporting equates to a Super Bowl every year."[11] The *John C. Stennis* arrived in 1998, with the *Chester Nimitz* and *Ronald Reagan* following early in the present century. The *Carl Vinson* was slated to replace the *Stennis,* thus keeping San Diego a three-carrier home port.

The cities, however, felt they were still owed sand by the navy. They needed it to protect beachside residences and lure tourists. The Silver Strand off affluent Coronado remained wide and stable, but poorer Imperial Beach, with surf crashing on the rock barrier in front of homes, was denuded. The sand supply from the nearby Tijuana River had been depleted by upstream dams, and the remaining flow of water from Mexico had become highly toxic. Carlsbad and Solana Beach were down to cobblestones. In Encinitas a woman had been killed in a landslide while sitting under a cliff on a narrow beach watching her husband surf. The round, concrete stubs of lifeguard stands were mute reminders of what the beaches had once been. There were no perches for lifeguards to look out at nonexistent bathers on nonexistent beaches. So the navy contributed sand dredged from six offshore sites. It was deposited on twelve beaches in San Diego County in 2001. The littoral drift and other natural forces began their work, and soon more sand was needed. The process seemed never-ending.

Meanwhile, the polluted bay remained just that. The National Oceanic and Atmospheric Administration (NOAA) had taken a look at twenty-three bays and estuaries throughout the nation and issued a report on the toxicity of their sediments. Newark Bay in New Jersey and San Diego Bay had the worst concentrations of chlorinated pesticides, PCBs, butyltins, PAHs, and metals. The toxicity patterns for the two bays were rated "pervasive." In San Diego Bay the toxicity of bottom sediments was particularly severe near the Thirty-second Street Naval Station and in several marinas and boat harbors.

When it took the samples in 1993 and issued the report five years later, NOAA worked closely with the Regional Water Quality Control Board, "which wanted to develop plans for the cleanup and remediation of toxic 'hot spots,' " the report stated.[12] The water quality control board initiated an action against the navy, its contractors, oil and utility companies, and the City of San Diego that has dragged on into the present century. The quality of water has remained the same, if not worse.

Both inside and outside the bay, sewage continues to pour into the waters of San Diego County causing gastroenteritis, dysentery, hepatitis, respiratory diseases, and other serious health problems. When Kelly Mayhew first went surfing in San Diego waters, he got sick about a half dozen times a year, "an ear thing or a stomach thing," he wrote.[13] The San Diego City College professor eventually adapted to the toxins, but he knew other surfers who had minor reactions or contracted serious blood diseases. Mayhew knows which beaches to avoid and checks the Internet for water quality readings before going surfing. When I was in San Diego, four million gallons of sewage poured into one of the rare undeveloped lagoons in Southern California. In conjunction with that event, the *San Diego Union-Tribune* listed ten major sewage spills since 2000. Beaches in the county are closed for hundreds of days each year, none more often than those in Imperial Beach that lie just north of the mouth of the Tijuana River.

The future lies beyond the city proper (or the proper city, as San Diegans would have it) and along the chaotic border, which is the southern portal into coastal California and a far different place from the northern entrance. The border area south of San Diego is partially within the city limits of "America's Finest City." It is, in fact, the conveniently forgotten underbelly of San Diego, and for that matter the

entire state. Dating back to the influx of Chinese laborers in the mid-nineteenth century, California has historically sought just the right number of people to serve its needs for cheap labor while, at the same time, attempting to bar excessive numbers. For a time, things got out of control along this section of the border.

The extreme southwestern corner of the United States feels menacing and looks desolate. This last section of coastline in California is a zone of horrors. It is an abandoned landscape, except for the nighttime scenes of constant warfare between a human tide of people inexorably walking north to seek better wages versus modern technological paraphernalia manned by humans who seek to deter them. This country has depended on such gadgets to fight its recent wars, and their innovation and production have greatly benefited a state dependent on the defense industry for its economic fixes.

The scene, which Alex and I visited and then revisited a number of times, is a mad mixture of a wasteland, toxic scum from NAFTA factories, untreated human wastes, live ammunition, badly eroded mesas, a struggling nature preserve harboring a national wildlife refuge, and a state park. This chaotic landscape is the dystopian present.

The odiferous Tijuana River, visible in the dry season because of the human refuse deposited along its course, is the most dominant feature. A study of where the river ends in the Tijuana Estuary just within the United States points out that the estuary has been diked, dredged, used as a dump and for sewage disposal, and mined for gravel. It asks the plausible question "Can any area that has experienced such extensive assaults still be considered a naturally functioning estuary?"[14]

Perhaps to give something of questionable value dignity, or to deny reality, the estuary has a number of imposing titles. The landform has been officially designated the Tijuana River National Estuarine Research Reserve, comprising the Tijuana Slough National Wildlife Refuge, Border Field State Park, and the Tijuana River Valley Open Space Preserve. Navy property, a state park, lands owned by the city and the county of San Diego, and private inholdings make up the fetid mix. Multiple dirt tracks used by illegal aliens and the Border Patrol crisscross the reserve–refuge–state park–open space preserve, and helicopters continually fly over it from an adjacent navy base known as "the Helicopter Capital of the World."

Arising in the Sierra de Juárez of northern Baja California and gathering intermittent flows from within its 1,735-square-mile watershed—three-fourths within Mexico and the remainder in the United States—the Tijuana River, enclosed between two angled concrete corsets, arcs gently westward from its northwest trending course at the international boundary, designated by yellow stripes on both sides of the concrete channel near the San Ysidro border crossing.

Extending east and west from the yellow lines and resembling the perimeter of a maximum security prison are a double fence, stadium-style lighting, infrared and television cameras, and magnetic and seismic sensors. On land, National Guard troops and visible Border Patrol agents are mounted on prosaic jeeps and more exotic horses, mountain bikes, four-wheel all-terrain vehicles called quads, and armored white 4x4 pickups with camper shells fitted out as detention cells. In the air and via the water, helicopters and fast watercraft varying from seventeen-foot inflatables to cigar-shaped, plastic-hulled vessels powered by engines that can propel them at speeds of up to sixty miles per hour zip around searching for illegal aliens.

The first time Alex and I walked the mile and a half from the dirt parking lot to the point where the border meets the ocean—the access road in the state park being closed because it was covered by toxic river water—we were treated to an impromptu exhibition of these deterrents: the multiple circular tire tracks incised in the beach sand by the quads, the helicopter that buzzed us, the two fast boats that played with the surf and nearly got caught by a rogue wave, and the two Border Patrol agents in knee-high boots standing stoically by their horse trailer. They reminded me of the African American cavalry troops stationed here during World War II.

It is people versus technology. The flow of people was partially stanched in 1994, when the first effective fence, called the primary fence, was constructed and more Border Patrol agents and modern technology were added. Before it had been a flood of people. Now it is a relative trickle, meaning about fifteen thousand arrests a year near the ocean, with an uncounted number making it through the various barriers. The total number illegally crossing the border is, however, the same—if not greater—because border crossings have shifted eastward, where there are fewer fences and border patrolmen but more natural hazards, such as dry mountains and hot deserts.

The first obstacle here, made of seven-foot-high Vietnam-era steel panels used for landing zones, is tattered—the decrepit victim of human batterings and natural landslides that have destroyed entire sections of fence. The panels are numbered to identify locations and are placed one to three feet north of the border to allow maintenance on the south side. By the time the fence reaches the beach at Las Playas de Tijuana, vertical steel rails coated to resist rust have replaced the panels. At the extreme end, the posts have been beaten into submission by the pounding surf.

The secondary fence, consisting of concrete columns spaced to allow wildlife to pass through but not illegal border crossers—unless they are equipped with jacks to spread the pillars—stopped 3.5 miles short of the beach when we were there. It is topped by an anticlimbing plate canted at a forty-five-degree angle. In accordance with the Secure Fence Act of 2006, the second fence will be extended 3.5 miles further and be accompanied by a massive leveling of two mesas that straddle Smugglers Gulch, in order to form a land bridge and make patrolling the border safer. (The second fence, along with extensive land grading and other deterrents, is new since our visit in 2008.) The steep-sided gulch, now a conduit for drugs, got its name for a different type of contraband transported during the Prohibition era.

The idea is to slow fence jumpers with the primary fence and catch them before they hop the second fence. The problem is that sometimes Border Patrol agents are caught between the two barriers with no quick exit, and their vehicles are pelted with bullets,

Molotov cocktails, stones, and ball bearings launched from slingshots. These assaults intended to kill or maim are also maneuvers to divert agents and allow others to slip across the border elsewhere. Abandoned in the dirt between the fences are single strands of steel rebar to which alternating steps have been welded to aid in the ascent of the fence. They are hooked at the end in order to catch onto the top of the fence.

If there is a will, there is a way. Before Operation Gatekeeper in 1994, people drove across the border on the beach. Now, walking at low tide, swimming, or paddling at night they come around the fence clutching plastic bags. They are clothed or in underclothes, bathing suits, or wetsuits. They may be walking in the surf, swimming unaided, or outfitted with flippers and face masks. They can be perched on surfboards, makeshift rafts, sailboats, or inner tubes towed across the international boundary by Jet Skis. They may be spotted on infrared scopes. If they make it past the cameras, lights, sensors, and agents they scamper up the beach or through the Tijuana Estuary, the channelized river having been loosened in its last few miles and allowed to flow freely when there is enough water to fill the meandering backwaters.

The river water, and the mud and dust when it is dry, contain industrial and domestic wastes from Tijuana. This thick brew is extremely toxic, enough to give Border Patrol agents respiratory problems, rashes, dizziness, and to eat the leather of their boots and synthetic gloves. A Web site maintained by the supporters of border patrolmen is particularly eloquent on this matter:

The border here is part of California's Border Field State Park. This is probably the only "park" on earth where sewage flows across it freely, where Ricin grows as a weed, and that is an uncleared bombing range.[15] This very real California State Park is so bad that the U.S. Border Patrol's labor union filed suit in the Federal Court of Claims seeking damages for its members who had to even stand in this place. The union received $15 million for the hundreds of members damaged by this place's fumes and fluids.[16]

The term used to describe this fetid watercourse is *blackwater river*. Human bodies, cars, refrigerators, tires, and plastic trash of every type litter the river, its banks, and its backwaters. A series of dark, fetid pools remains after the flows cease. A sewage treatment plant on the U.S. side of the border treats only wastes generated in the dry season. If the river's current is strong enough, it will flow through the twenty-five-hundred-acre estuary to the ocean, where the contaminated waters will be dispersed by offshore currents and wafted north to Imperial Beach and San Diego beaches and south to the beaches of Tijuana and Rosarito Beach. At the end of Seacoast Drive in Imperial Beach, there is a sign that can be flipped either way, depending on daily conditions: Enjoy the Beach: Keep It Clean. Or: Danger Contaminated Water: Avoid Water Contact from This Point South to the International Border.

Tijuana Sloughs, a fabled—or "mysto" in surfer parlance—big-wave surfing spot described along with the border area in Kem Nunn's novel *Tijuana Straits*, sits one mile offshore of the entrance to the estuary. Nunn wrote of the fence that stretches across the beach: "The huge fence loomed above her, repository of crosses, the names of the dead—the infamous fence. In Las Playas they died among its narrow pilings on a regular basis, pinned there like so many exotic insects by the powerful currents that swept the beach."[17] To Nunn, the estuary was a place of reeking, sulfurous evil.

Pioneer surfers discovered the Tijuana Sloughs in the 1930s, and some of the surfing greats like Dempsey Holder, Bob Simmons, and Buzzy Trent have ridden these big waves. Because of the pollution, a hepatitis shot is recommended nowadays. Sharks, killer whales, sets of sneaker waves, water the color of milk chocolate, debris from Tijuana, and a long paddle to the cobblestone reefs mean that only the most venturesome big-wave surfers on long boards are attracted to the Tijuana Sloughs. A strong northwest wind generates huge swells in winter, the season when the surfing is best, but also the time when the water is most polluted because of the wastes washed downstream by the rain.

Besides water pollution, there are the constant reminders of preparations for seemingly never-ending warfare. The *whomp, whomp, whomp* of helicopters circling counterclockwise and practicing landings rises from the nearby navy airfield. A half dozen choppers circle and dip their tails in simulated landings and then repeat the maneuver again and again and again. In World War II, gunnery and bombing practice were conducted here and coastal batteries protected the local beaches and the entrance to distant San Diego Harbor.

But the huge surge of illegal aliens rolling across the border at this point, trampling rare plants and endangered bird nests and sucking the content of the birds' eggs for sustenance, has lessened in the last fifteen years. Imperial Beach has given up plans for a marina in the estuary and a pricy land development named Monument City. Property values have increased in Imperial Beach. When the second fence is extended toward the ocean and more agents and newer technology are added, the cities of Imperial Beach and San Diego, the state of California, and its coastline will become more insular.

51. *(Previous page)* Crowd barricade in surf. Ocean Beach, San Francisco, 2005.

52. *(Above)* Truck tire in sand. Ocean Beach, San Francisco, 2007.

53. *(Right)* Sag pond covering the San Andreas Fault. Fort Ross, 2009.

54. Dead sea lion, one of hundreds washed up on beaches as a result of starvation, an apparent consequence of climatic changes. McClures Beach, Point Reyes, 2009.

55. School of sardines, a species once fished to near extinction, on display in aquarium tank. Monterey Bay Aquarium, 2010.

56. Fishing boat salvage yard overflowing after collapse of salmon stock. Noyo, Fort Bragg, 2007.

57. *(Previous spread)* Nuclear carriers and San Diego skyline. San Diego, 2010.

58. *(Above)* Condo development under construction. Long Beach, 2007.

59. *(Right)* Jen, a bass guitarist for a surf punk band. Pillar Point Harbor, Half Moon Bay, 2008.

60. "Fire for Effect," a sign on a Nike missile radar installation, now in ruins. Wolf Ridge, Sausalito, 2006.

61. Missile Park. Naval Air Weapons Station, Point Mugu, 2007.

62. Surfers in fog waiting for waves. Huntington Beach, 2008.

63. Sewage outfall pipe. Fort Funston, San Francisco, 2005.

64. *(Above)* BP oil refinery and giant flag. Long Beach, 2009.

65. *(Right)* USS *Ronald Reagan*. San Diego, 2010.

66. Reporter for a TV celebrity news show in front of ruins left by a church fire. Malibu, 2007.

67. Photo shoot for a mobile phone advertisement; a controversial fence restricting beach access stands in the background. Malibu Beach Colony, 2007.

68.*(Above)* View of chapel through leaded glass window of Russian settlers' residence. Fort Ross State Historic Park, 2006.

69.*(Right)* Historical Events in the Life of This Tree, AD 100 to AD 1943. Section of an ancient redwood tree trunk on display. Fort Bragg, 2007.

HISTORICAL EVENTS IN
LIFE OF THIS TREE

AD

0. 190 TREE STARTED AS SEEDLING

1. 215 FIRST YEAR OF THIS SECTION

2. 311 CHRISTIANITY RECOGNIZED LEGALLY

3. 395 ROMAN EMPIRE DIVIDED

4. 632 BEGINNING OF MOHAMMEDANISM

5. 800 CHARLEMAGNE BECAME EMPEROR OF THE WEST

6. 962 HOLY ROMAN EMPIRE RESTORED

7. 1066 NORMANS CONQUER ENGLAND

8. 1118 ORDER OF KNIGHTS TEMPLAR FOUNDED

9. 1215 MAGNA CHARTA SIGNED

10. 1295 MARCO POLO RETURNED TO VENICE

11. 1492 COLUMBUS DISCOVERED AMERICA

12. 1542 CABRILLO DISCOVERED CALIFORNIA FROM SEA

13. 1632 GUSTAVUS II, GREAT SWEDISH KING, DIED

14. 1776 DECLARATION OF INDEPENDENCE

15. 1851 FIRST SAWMILL IN MENDOCINO COUNTY

16. 1885 C.R. JOHNSON BUILT SAWMILL AT FORT BRAGG

17. 1943 YEAR THIS TREE WAS CUT

70. *(Left)* Tijuana Estuary and circling Blackhawk helicopters. Imperial Beach, 2010.

71. *(Above)* David on his farm, with free-range, grass-fed cows. Point Reyes, 2008.

72. Shopping bag, front and back. Santa Monica Beach, 2008.

73. Two men standing in front of gun battery. Battery Wallace, Fort Barry, Marin Headlands, 2008.

74. *(Previous spread)* Port of Los Angeles. San Pedro, 2008.

75. *(Right)* Tourists from Taiwan. Yerba Buena Island, 2005.

76. *(Right)* Dad napping on beach, and passing aircraft. Dockweiler State Beach, 2007.

77. *(Following page)* On the edge. Fort Funston, San Francisco, 2010.

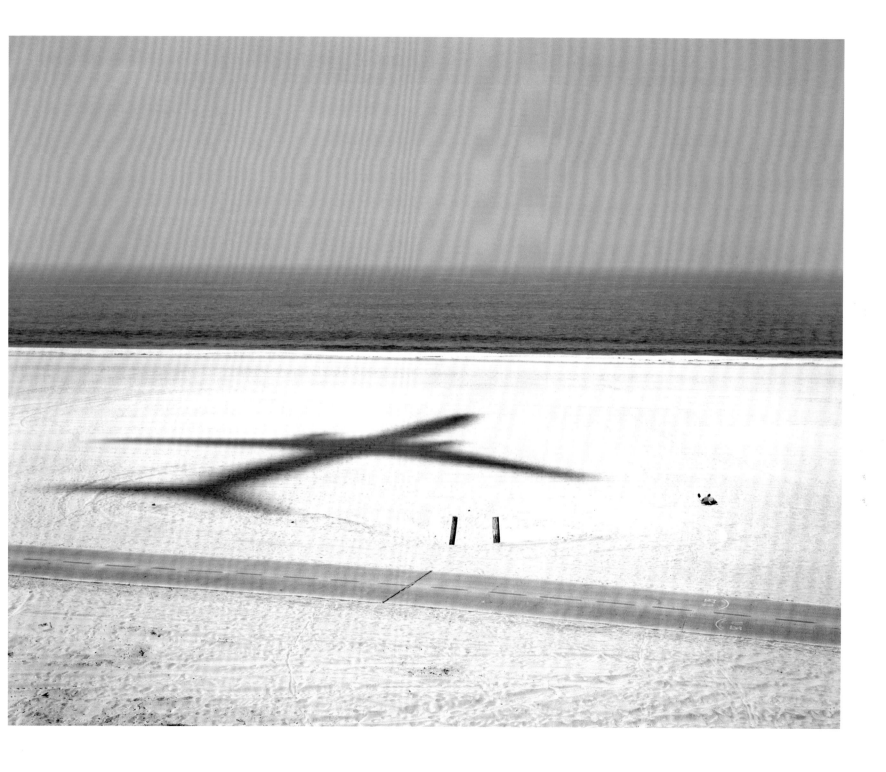

From Newport Landing to Point Fermin, nearly 20 miles, the coast is low with several lagoons in the vicinity of the beach. . . . The country is treeless, except in the valleys and gulches, and is covered with grass and sagebrush, green during the rainy season, but brown in summer. **United States Coast Pilot,** 1909

THE POLITICAL COAST

Along the water's edge around Huntington Beach (20 alt., 2,690 pop.), rise bleak oil derricks. Before oil was discovered here after 1920, the town had developed as a minor recreational resort, but local residents profited little, having sold most of their holdings before the discovery was known. The buying campaign had gone on so quietly that few were aware of the unusual number of sales. The tidelands here have remained State property but oil operators have developed a new technique of drilling to meet the situation; from their land, the former town lots, they drill on a bias [slant drilling] to tap the pools under the tidelands. The practice has stirred up one of the State's bitterest controversies. **The WPA Guide to California,** 1939

The 20-mile coast from Newport Bay to Point Fermin is low, and there are several lagoons near the beach. There are no trees near the shore; towns and resorts are almost continuous along the beach. **United States Coast Pilot,** 2006

For the first time in 107 years, the tide is flowing again into parts of the wetlands that had been cut off from the ocean. The result is a revitalized ecosystem, a return of native plants and improved habitat for fish and shorebirds, including nesting endangered species. **Huntington Beach Visitors Guide,** 2008

The California coast has been shaped not only by natural forces and the works of humans but also by laws, primarily the initiative measure known as Proposition 20 passed by voters in 1972, and its follow-on, the California Coastal Act of 1976, enacted by the legislature and signed by the governor. The act, somewhat amended, remains the toughest, most comprehensive land use law in the country, with jurisdiction over its most varied, extensive, and valuable piece of real estate. The law and its implementation by the California Coastal Commission sets the planning standards and regulatory practices for the coast. For example, it is the principal means whereby a degraded wetland can be restored to something approximating its original condition. The process of wetland restoration, whether it be the few acres on the edge of San Pedro Bay or the hundreds of acres at the end of Tomales Bay, has become a cottage industry in California, albeit one with great potential for growth because of past human impacts.

The Bolsa Chica wetlands in Orange County morphed over the life of the Coastal Commission from a swamp (more politely known as a marsh) into a viable wetland and finally an ecological reserve, its current official status. The thirty years it took to span those extremes involved oil companies, residential developers, environmentalists, ports, and every city, county, state, and federal government agency that had anything remotely to do with this section of the coastline. The length of time, the costs, the complexity of the relationships between the many players, and the qualified success they achieved is an excellent example of the politics of coastline protection and the role of the California Coastal Commission.

What is a "qualified success"? Without the Coastal Act and the Coastal Commission, there is no doubt the 1,318-acre Bolsa Chica Ecological Reserve would not exist today in its present form. Acquiring the reserve, and restoring nearly half of the total acreage to full or partial wetland status, cost more than $270 million. In its place there would have been some variation of the massive residential, commercial, and marina complex and the token wetland proposed in the early 1970s. That development would have been accompanied by a corresponding increase in population, traffic, and peripheral commercial ventures along the Pacific Coast Highway between Huntington Harbour and Huntington Beach, which is now open space. To the east there is a solid wall of houses and inland Orange County. To the west there is Huntington State Beach, offshore oil platforms, Catalina Island, and the Pacific Ocean. Within the reserve, there is relative calm and wildlife.

The wetland is an imperfect island within a vast sea of development. True, the restoration gained much-needed open space and wildlife habitat, but it resembles the raw land of a harbor complex under construction minus the tall cranes. The aesthetics seem to have been borrowed from the ports of Los Angeles and Long Beach, who supplied $102 million as mitigation for their similar-looking landfills in San Pedro Bay. There are high barbed-wire fences protecting snowy plover nesting areas from unleashed dogs whose owners don't heed signs, bare and eroded slopes on which new plants have atrophied, walls of rock armoring the sides of the tidal basin that resemble the attempts to ward off ocean encroachment on nearby coastal beaches, ten tons of trash and debris deposited on a yearly basis in the ecological reserve from a flood control channel, oil wells nodding constantly in the background, the monotone of traffic along the busy coastal highway, and expensive homes on the bluffs overlooking the reserve whose picture windows reflect the glare of the vivid sunsets on the western horizon.

Restoration, however, is relative, meaning it is in the eyes of the beholder and is shaped by the culture within which it occurs, in this case coastal Orange County, where there was no possibility of a pristine solution, as there is in Northern California. There is just too much existing on the ground and in people's minds and pocketbooks in Southern California to achieve a purely natural result. At the conclusion there were fewer oil wells, fewer new homes, and more acres of wetlands. The restoration of Bolsa Chica is a classic example of confrontation, compromise, and resolution—all hallmarks of the modus operandi of the Coastal Commission.

A fairly sophisticated Native American presence once existed along the edge of the Bolsa Chica Mesa. They chose the site because of the vista, the same reason the developer of what came to be known as Brightwater located homes above the wetland. For the Gabrielino and Juaneno tribal groups and their predecessors, the view from the mesa helped determine the seasons. During three days in late December, the sun sets over West End Point on Catalina Island, indicating the winter solstice. The sun sets directly over San Pedro Hill during the spring and fall equinoxes. Bones and artifacts helped date the presence of Native Americans on Bolsa Chica Mesa to a period lasting from eight to three thousand years ago, making it the earliest reliably dated astronomical observatory site in North America.

The surrounding natural resources were ideal for a permanent population. There were freshwater seeps and springs. On occasion the Santa Ana River, which made wide swings across the landscape, flowed through the Bolsa Chica Gap and mixed with salt water gushing through a natural tidal inlet into twenty-three hundred acres of irregularly configured lagoons and marshlands. Over a hundred thousand artifacts, dense concentrations of human and animal bones and shells, and rare semisubterranean pit houses were uncovered during archeological excavations for the Brightwater subdivision. Hundreds of cogged stones were also discovered. The round or oval-shaped stones have grooves incised in their edges, causing them to resemble gears. Stones like these are also found in Chile. What has been uncovered, where homes costing up to $3 million have been constructed, indicates the prior existence of an advanced Native American culture.

The use and ownership of the land passed, as it did elsewhere along the California coast, from the Native Americans to the Spanish, Mexicans, and Anglos. An Anglo gained title to the land from a Mexican. The uplands were grazed and farmed and the lagoons were fished. Then in the 1890s came the first significant alteration of the landscape, with the establishment of the Bolsa Chica Gun Club by wealthy Los Angeles businessmen. The club blocked the ocean inlet and built tidal gates to create freshwater for hunting and agricultural purposes. Dikes were built, the land drained, and smaller farm parcels created. What had been undulating fingers of marshland became fists of clogged water. A strip of marsh edged with pickleweed just back of the coastal sand dunes was left relatively untouched and remains the first visible and most pristine component of the wetland today.

The transition from a relatively wild land to farmland to an industrial landscape was sudden. Beginning in the 1920s, oil drilling and its resulting industrial blight spread across the wetland. More than 430 oil wells and their associated roads, pipelines, and tank farms were located on the lowlands at the height of production. There are now 200 wells in the Huntington Beach Field, described by its current owner as "one of the most prolific oil producing regions for its geographic size in the world."[1] The oil wells are present because they predated passage of the coastal initiative and act. Over the years there have been a number of owners of the field, including Signal Oil Company. The most recent is Aera Energy, jointly owned by Shell and ExxonMobil. Crude oil and natural gas from the land-based wells, and from Platform Emmy located 1.3 miles offshore, are processed onsite. Production on the reserve will continue for as long as the field produces oil and gas, estimated to be a matter of decades.

In 1970 Signal Oil began diversifying into land development. It purchased 2,000 acres from the heirs of the gun club, retained the surface rights, and sold the mineral rights to another oil company. The owners of the surface and mineral rights went through a number of corporate, management, and personnel

changes during the forty-year span of what the *Los Angeles Times* has repeatedly referred to as "the tortured tale of Bolsa Chica." Signal Landmark Corporation exchanged land with the State Lands Commission, giving the relatively pristine 320 acres bordering the sand dunes to the state and keeping 1,700 acres. State lands extend to the mean high-tide mark, but the meandering tidal line of the marsh had never been accurately surveyed. The trade squared the boundaries, thus giving Signal more developable land.

Plans for the 5,700-unit residential-marina-commercial development on 1,547 acres were announced. The Bolsa Chica marsh became the local cause célèbre for the passage of Proposition 20. Concerned Huntington Beach citizens gathered signatures for the initiative during the height of environmental concern ignited by the 1969 Santa Barbara oil spill and the first Earth Day in 1970. Ballona and Upper Newport Bay wetlands had similar "friends" groups.

Those Huntington Beach residents who wanted to save Bolsa Chica organized themselves under the name of the Amigos de Bolsa Chica in 1976, the same year the Coastal Act was passed making permanent the statewide and regional commissions created by the 1972 initiative. For thirty years, to 2006, when water poured into the wetland through a tidal inlet for the first time in more than a century, Amigos was the dominant environmental organization seeking to find an alternative to large-scale development. Its members thoroughly researched and presented their findings in a reasonable manner. Signal Landmark relied on its greater monetary resources to gain the support of most county supervisors and state legislators. "The advantage the private sector had over a group like Amigos—and they had advantages we didn't—is that we could throw money at an election," said a senior vice president of Signal. "They could gain the grassroots support, and we couldn't." Deadlock ensued. Decision makers grew tired of hearing the same arguments from each side. At the end of the process there was the Coastal Commission, something that was not lost on either party. One of the presidents of Amigos, who was a lawyer, said, "We had the coastal act, and that's what we were working through, and, of course, they were trying to amend the coastal act."[2]

The assertion of the public's rights in the early 1970s that resulted in the passage of the Coastal Act shifted in the early 1980s to protecting private property rights. Nowhere else was that change more noticeable than in Republican Orange County, where property rights regained their sacred status. The Amigos float was not allowed in a July Fourth parade because it contained what the Huntington Beach Parade Committee determined was a political word. *Wetland* had negative connotations in that environment, just as it was a term of approbation elsewhere. The floats of the Republican Women of Huntington Harbour and the Democratic Council of West Orange County were allowed to participate. At the state level, Republican Governor George Deukmejian, who was from neighboring Long Beach, slashed the Coastal Commission's budget, resulting in the loss of staff, one regional office, push-button telephones, and computers.

The Coastal Commission staff was attuned to the wider contexts within which it operated. Over the years it had adapted its operations to political and legal realities in order to survive the wrath of governors and crippling legislative amendments. At a luncheon meeting with members of Amigos, Peter Douglas, the commission's executive director, "made it very clear that he felt they could not prevent all development on the lowlands or the wetlands, only some development."[3] Douglas added that the prohibition of all development would qualify as an unconstitutional taking of private property.

Douglas, the commission's longtime executive director, who coauthored Proposition 20, was a practical as well as a spiritual believer in protecting the coast. He endured setbacks with the equanimity of a Zen bureaucrat. Douglas was, in short, an anomaly in government. He was a survivor committed to a cause. I've known Peter since the early 1970s, when he handled coastal bills in the legislature and I wrote about them for the *Los Angeles Times*. A member of his staff, who had worked for the commission for a quarter-century, said, "It's not the battle but the war Peter is aware of."

Besides a constant lack of sufficient funds for the independent regulatory agency that rules on projects covering a broad range of social and economic interests often in the multimillion-dollar range, Douglas has had to work with both good and bad commissions over the years. The twelve commissioners are appointed equally by the governor, the Speaker of the Assembly, and the Senate Rules Committee. Through the years they have voted on the merits of a matter, in accordance with their personal agendas, or at the behest of their appointing authorities. One way to soften the political impact of a decision is to give approval with conditions, which may improve or may sink a project. A Signal Landmark attorney described the coastal political process as "a twilight zone time."[4]

Against this background, the commission adopted the first plan for development of Bolsa Chica. The 1985 staff report began: "The history of planning for Bolsa Chica has been long, complex, and controversial."[5] Little did the staff realize there was still a long way to go. The plan called for massive development, but it had conditions. There would be a 5,700-unit residential development on 500 acres; 1,300 boat slips in a 75-acre marina/commercial development; a wide, navigable ocean inlet; a road bisecting the wetlands; and a 150-room hotel. In exchange, Signal Landmark had to provide 915 acres of "high quality" wetlands. That meant cleaning up the oil pollution on property owned by another oil company that wanted no part of the transaction. The adoption of the Bolsa Chica Land Use Plan, which stood for ten years as an approximation of the commission's thinking on the subject, stirred up a lot of public controversy.

Amigos scored a public relations coup on the marina issue. The public was invited to the north end of the beach at the point where it met Huntington Harbour. That was the proposed location of the inlet on which the marina depended. Hot dogs and soft drinks were served. More than six hundred people showed up and stood shoulder to shoulder for a distance of 700 feet between two vertical lines of black paper representing the two proposed breakwaters. The parallel breakwaters would have lined the pro-

posed inlet, forming its sides. The organizers hired an airplane to fly over and take photographs. The Hands Across the Sand event made the Los Angeles evening television news.

A lawsuit against Signal Oil was costing Amigos a lot of money, the oil company foresaw additional costs, a new management team was willing to explore fresh approaches, and the regulatory agencies were tired of hearing the same arguments. There needed to be movement. Representatives of Amigos, Signal, the State Lands Commission, Orange County, and the City of Huntington Beach met in November 1988. A coalition was formed and a mediator hired. It took the principals six months to agree on a conceptual plan. The plan, however, had no official status. Government agencies, including the Coastal Commission, would determine what was allowable.

More detailed plans bounced back and forth between the city, county, and Coastal Commission during the 1990s. The most controversial issue was the construction of nine hundred homes on the lower portion of the property, which meant filling 120 acres of the wetlands and eliminating environmentally sensitive habitats. In return, Signal would pay for the restoration of 770 acres of wetlands. Full build-out of twenty-five hundred homes on the mesa would be allowed. The Coastal Commission approved the filling of the wetlands and destruction of sensitive habitats, which was not its finest hour.

The Bolsa Chica Land Trust then filed suit, and the court said residential use of the lowlands was not allowed under provisions of the Coastal Act. The commission reversed its previous action, an easy matter since the ports of Los Angeles and Long Beach had since ridden to the rescue and provided $89.5 million to purchase and partially restore 892 acres of wetland. Of the total, 377 acres would be restored to full tidal wetlands, and 240 acres to partial or "muted" wetlands. The downside was that, in order to get the mitigation credits that the ports needed to fill San Pedro Bay, dredging of the wetlands had to extend deeper than the biologists would have liked. The upside was that the ports provided funding for two bridges on the coast highway that spanned a narrow tidal inlet incised in the state beach on the south side of the reserve. The inlet supplied the ocean water needed to flush the deeper basins. Nearly 300 acres would continue as an oil field until there was no more oil for Aera Energy to extract. At that point, phase two of the restoration would be undertaken, which would require additional funding and permits far into the future.[6]

The number of homes permitted on the mesa, and the acreage on which they could be built, shrank until it reached 349 houses on 68 acres, far better than the original 5,700 units on 1,547 acres. Although restoring Bolsa Chica took a long time, cost many millions of dollars, and is yet to be completed, it reflected the moderating nature of coastal politics.

When I visited Brightwater during the great housing recession at the end of the last decade, business was slow. But the view at sunset, with a full moon rising in the east, was incredible, as it must also have been for the Gabrielino Indians. The wetlands were a dark hole in an otherwise illuminated residential landscape. The lights of commuter traffic heading toward homes similar to those in Brightwater were a vivid stream along the Pacific Coast Highway. In the distance, the navigation lights of a container ship plowing toward Asia were visible. I was proud to have been a small part of this political process and pleased that this trip along the entirety of the California Coast had again been made with Alex, who now directed our vehicle homeward.

PHOTOGRAPHER'S AFTERWORD ALEX FRADKIN

Until I began photographing the California coast for this project, I hadn't thought it would be so difficult to define. It was simply "home," the place where some of my earliest and most evocative memories were formed, and where I was from. Some part of the coast was always my destination when I wanted to play, relax, discover, and escape. It was a specific and constant geography, always accessible, always yielding its intense beauty and revealing its diverse, unpredictable temperament.

Like my dad, I have always lived near the water. I was born in Los Angeles, and after my parents divorced, when I was four, I moved with my mom to San Francisco. In the early seventies, I traveled with my dad when he was researching his first book on the coast. Many of my first enduring recollections of this place were formed during that trip. As the years continue to separate the Then from the Now, those early memories get mixed with imagination and the layers of time. Some memories stay intact; others morph into narratives in which fiction and fact can be at odds. But that's not unusual. This left edge of the continent has always inspired the fusion of myth and reality. This is a well-trodden subject, but one I had not yet fully engaged with until I began my own journey of inquiry with my camera for this book.

My great-grandparents on my mother's side came to California in the 1800s in covered wagons, surviving disease and hunger and coping with the ever present fear of being attacked by Indians. Eventually they settled in the central Sacramento Valley, becoming cattle farmers. To a limited extent, their sacrifices and risks paid off, and they prospered. My dad came to California from the East Coast in 1960, and has spent the past fifty years tilling the literary soil of California and the West. Both sides of my family were seeking something. Both became involved in the landscape of California in their own ways. My great-grandparents farmed the soil, and my Dad wrote about the land, titling his first book *California: The Golden Coast,* his own reference to this mythical place.

Until I set out with a camera to photograph my home in its entirety, I never recognized how complex this coastal region is. The prospect of photographing its disparate parts and creating a cohesive body of images was daunting: it is made up of more than one thousand miles of coastline composed of widely varying landscapes, cultures, social classes, and ethnic groups, each region loaded with its own history, its own story to tell. It is a place where memory, perception, history, imagination, and fact collide, momentarily align, and then fracture apart again. There is not one California coast but many.

My dad, having tackled large and overwhelming subjects before, suggested a categorical approach to make the project more digestible and focused. This worked as a structural device for the first year. Increasingly I moved away from it, however, as I continued to be drawn to a more nuanced, ambiguous, and reflective depiction. As I veered from the prescribed path, a few spirited conversations ensued, but in the end we both felt that our unique voices and interpretations would make for a stronger body of work, one that combined our respective generational viewpoints in words and pictures.

I began the project by revisiting the efforts of Edward Weston, Ansel Adams, and Minor White, among others, examining how they had previously photographed this coast. Any thoughts I had about following in their footsteps were quickly abandoned. *That* coast no longer existed, a point brought into stark focus when I visited Point Lobos. There were parking lots jammed with RVs, and tourists everywhere, crawling over the tide pools, crowding the pathways, and tramping past warning signs that implored hikers to preserve the fragile landscape. Oceano Dunes, another favorite Weston haunt, has fared far worse over time. All-terrain vehicles buzzing like angry wasps were carving up the dunes and erasing the natural wind-sculpted forms that Weston had once photographed with such exquisite attention to light and form.

Midway through the project, I noticed while looking through my images that I had begun to develop an emotional response to this landscape rather than a strict representational view. I have always tended to work an idea over and over with images, repeatedly revisiting a location and shaping it into compliance with a preformed design by strictly choosing my light, composition, and subject matter. But during the course of this project, I learned to relax this stylistic rigidity and let ambiguity and curiosity guide me, even if doing so put me in opposition to the original program. The coast, my subconscious, and my intuition conspired to challenge the idea that a single photographic narrative with a categorical view of the coast's various parts could represent the landscape in its entirety. Simply put, the project became more personal. I was no longer a dispassionate observer but a participant in this landscape—a place where I was a native and in which I had formed my first perceptions of the natural environment, a place I was still seeking to belong to.

Guided by my curiosity, my memories, and chance, I surrendered myself and my camera to whatever was both unexpected and compelling. Often when I returned to a particular location with a specific image in mind, the unpredictable coast would yield something else, something different, better—or sometimes something completely unworkable. I was subject to the capriciousness of the coast and what *it* intended.

And what I found was beauty and tranquility, death and danger, which occur close together on the coastal edge. These contradictions are hard to reconcile and sometimes become intertwined. Fires, earthquakes, landslides, crimes, drownings, and falls from cliffs happen here repeatedly, and yet so many who come to walk along the shore seek inner peace.

The cycle of life, too, with its complex interrelationships, plays itself out over and over along the coast. Birds, seals, and other kinds of wildlife begin and end their lives here. It is not uncommon to come upon parts of beaches cordoned off during the nesting season for migrating birds, or designated birthing areas for seals, with signs warning people away from the sensitive habitats. At the opposite end of the life cycle, seal carcasses, when washed up on the shore partially eaten or decomposed, sometimes leave a ghoulish menagerie in the sand. Their remains provide nutrients to other species in a complex system that continually reminds me that all things are interrelated and the cycle continues.

The fragility of life and of its rhythmic succession became disturbingly clear for me in the late spring of 2009, when starving and sick sea lions began washing up on the shore of the Northern California coast. News accounts reported the cause of death as starvation, in part the result of changing water tem-

peratures caused by global warming, which had forced the sea lions' food sources to move north to cooler waters. Something similar had happened only a few months earlier, when hundreds of cormorants had washed up on the beaches, dead and dying from malnourishment. I found these deaths deeply chilling. If this was not a natural phenomenon, then it was likely a harbinger of worse things to come. Despite the epic grandeur of our coast, its seeming timelessness, it is not impervious to the harm caused by centuries of abuse to a delicate ecosystem. This is sadly evident in the rapidly dwindling populations of salmon and other species native to the coast, in the near disappearance of the last few stands of old growth redwoods, and in the effects of a rapidly growing urbanscape too close to the edge. The vast majority of California's huge population lives within a few miles of the coast, which inevitably adds to the stresses placed on this landscape.

While I worked on this book, the country was, as it still is, at war. In the past, California's fortifications faced out to sea, anticipating the enemy that never came. Decaying remnants of bunkers, signs of past preparation for war, still stand along the coast from border to border. But visible signs of present-day vigilance, too, are everywhere, primarily focused on the terrorist threat overseas and the "enemy within." I was questioned repeatedly when photographing near "sensitive" areas. Each time, my ID, project documentation, and supporting materials were scrutinized. When I explained the purpose of my project, the officer would look at where my camera was pointed and ask what I was finding of interest there. His suspicious tone seemed to ask, "If you're taking pictures for a book on the California coast, why aren't you photographing the sunset or the pretty beach?"

In contrast, the overwhelming response that I received from most individuals I met along the coast was one of complete openness and very little suspicion or protectiveness. Shifting from observer to participant, I overcame my hesitation and asked people to become part of this project by letting me photograph them. The extraordinary social and ethnic diversity of those I talked to and photographed gave me a perspective I had not anticipated. I discovered during the course of explaining my work, and the long process of setting up my view camera, focusing, and loading the film holder, that strangers would reveal who they were and what this coast meant to them. When the moment came to take the picture, they would freeze, give me the pose they wished to project, and silently gaze at me as I stood behind the camera. My presence was affirmed both in the landscape where we stood and in their consciousness, and the resulting image registered their existence and gave them a place in the project that lives on in this nar-rative. It was a mutual and fulfilling exchange. We both mattered.

The unifying element of this project was the coast's contradictions and its refusal to be coherently deciphered or depicted. Coastal California is easy to imagine, hard to hold, and impossible to fully describe, and it is precisely this peculiarity that keeps me intrigued with this special place. My curiosity is far from satisfied, and twenty years from now I will still be asking questions and taking pictures. I want to share the coast with the children my wife and I plan to raise here. I will introduce them, as my father did for me, to a place they can always think of as both familiar and mysterious, a place that will be a source of their memories and dreams.

I hope that in this book you will see at least a little of *your* California coast. A mood, a glimpse of something you remember from when you spent time along this shore—that you will have a visceral, emotional response that reestablishes that precious link of place to person and feel the interconnectedness, if only for a moment.

Philip and Alex Fradkin. Mattole Beach campground, Lost Coast, 2009. Photos by Alex Fradkin.

ACKNOWLEDGMENTS

ALEX FRADKIN

The process of making a compelling photograph is in large part about access and collaboration, as well as about knowing where to aim the camera, lighting, skill, and luck. In my five years of wandering up and down the California coast, I met many people who allowed me into their homes, patiently posed while I took their portraits, and shared parts of their lives with me. I am forever grateful to them for their trust and generosity.

I am deeply indebted to and thank the following individuals and organizations: Sheila Levine and Jenny Wapner, our editors at University of California Press, for supporting our vision for the project and making it happen; Jean Brotherton, for her wonderful and warm hospitality while I stayed in her home; Trisha Malahni, who secured our access to the Los Angeles Harbor; Lt. Sean Riordan and Lt. Aaron Kakiel of the U.S. Navy; Jenny Slafkosky of the Monterey Bay Aquarium, and Kim Fulton-Bennett of the Monterey Bay Aquarium Research Institute.

I am deeply grateful for the love and encouragement of my friends and colleagues, who supported me emotionally, helped guide me, made suggestions, and generally were "there" during the ups and downs of this long project. In particular, I thank Dave and Kristi Shearer, Eric Unger, John Ranucci, Dan and Tatiana Brotherton, Greg and Ilene Snyder, and Heather and Mark Mahaney.

I greatly appreciate the few remaining independent photographic film suppliers and processing labs who support photographic artists. In particular, Michael Pazdon and Ryan Hendon of Lightwaves; Rob Rieter, owner of Lightroom; and the fantastic staff at

Looking Glass Photo and Camera Supply, all located in Berkeley. Film is not dead!

I owe everything to my family, who, without hesitation, thought it was a natural and logical decision for me to drop my former profession as an architect and pick up a camera to explore the world. My mom, an unwavering vital force of love and support in my life, is an inspiration in so many ways. Mom introduced me to the wonders and mysteries of a diverse planet, taking me everywhere with her and instilling a deep love of adventure and curiosity. My grandmother Missy gave me my first camera and was the first in the family to "go digital." She is closing in fast on her one-hundredth birthday and is still picking up speed and forever cheering me on. My "other mom," Patricia Snyder, has always made her home and presence a comfortable and warm place to be, a sanctuary from the storms.

And I thank my dad, who first proposed the idea of doing a project together. When I was a young child, he took me everywhere with him, introducing me to his great love of landscape and place, imbuing the coast with warm memories for me. Many years ago, he was instrumental in pushing through legislation that helped protect the California coastline, which made it possible for others to create such memories. I will always think of him when standing on the shoreline. My mom gave me the world beyond my home, and Dad gave me the world right here in my backyard.

Last, but foremost and most personal, I thank my brilliant and beautiful wife, Marina, who joined me in life and partnership late in the project. Our first date was spent at Point Reyes, where we later got married on a bluff overlooking Tomales Bay. Together we explored the California coast, forming new memories of a different and wonderful kind. Love, life, and passion on the shores of this incredible place gave me a new and needed perspective, influenced my vision, and forever changed me in ways yet to be fully discovered.

PHILIP FRADKIN

Researching this book was like visiting old friends with new faces. After thirty-five years between books on the coast, I found that the places were recognizable but the people who were knowledgeable about them had changed. The following are some of the people who helped me along the way with my topics, from north to south: Al Mikkelsen on the Wild Coast: Carola DeRooy, Dewey Livingston, Elizabeth Ptak, and Ellie Rilla on the Agricultural Coast; Earl E. Brabb and Gary Griggs on the Residential Coast; Ken Peterson and John Sanders on the Tourist Coast; Shelly Butler, Amber Copilow, and Jim Harris on the Recreational Coast; Arley Baker, Cindy Betz, Richard Crowley, Gene Harris, and Kirk Marckwald on the Industrial Coast; Navy Lt. Amy Carmickle, Border Patrol Agent Damon Foreman, Richard J. Seymour, and Abraham J. Shragge on the Military Coast; and Shirley Dettloff, Peter Douglas, Michael J. Fischer, and Teresa Henry on the Political Coast. I owe a special debt of gratitude to Peter Douglas for guiding me through the intricacies of Sacramento in the 1970s, for submitting to two interviews, and for what he has achieved in terms of coastal protection.

I also thank the editors of the Arcadia Publishing Company for keeping the histories of minute areas alive in the form of a series of paperback books with carefully selected black-and-white photographs, short texts, and captions written by knowledgeable local historians. Some history, especially if it is easily digestible, is better than no history—a condition California excels in—and perhaps Arcadia will act as a bridge between the print and electronic eras.

My son, Alex, who kept saying "I hear you, Dad" when I suggested certain photographs and then shot the photograph he wanted, was again a wonderful presence. I had the pleasure of his near-constant company until he fell in love, the only excuse I would tolerate for his absence. His wife, Marina Sitrin, was a great addition to the team.

Doris Ober and Dianne Fradkin read the entire manuscript. Dewey Livingston, Elizabeth Ptak, and Peter Douglas read parts of it before I submitted it to Jenny Wapner, the environmental studies editor at the University of California Press, who caught the remaining infelicitous phrases. I am, of course, ultimately responsible for all the words. Kim Robinson took the project over when Jenny departed, and Dore Brown once again shepherded one of my books through production. I also thank Sheila Levine, who has guided me through the intricacies of UC Press for the past few years. Now back to work on the next book I am due to deliver to the press.

NOTES

COASTAL MEMORIES

1. Philip L. Fradkin, *California: The Golden Coast* (New York: Viking, 1974), 108.

2. Ibid., 105.

THE WILD COAST

Epigraphs: Coast and Geodetic Survey, *United States Coast Pilot, Pacific Coast* (Washington, D.C.: Government Printing Office, 1909), 100; J. Smeaton Chase, *California Coast Trails: A Horseback Ride From Mexico to Oregon* (Boston: Houghton Mifflin, 1913), 310; Gladys Ayer Nomland, "The Flood," in *Sinkyone Notes,* University of California Publications in American Archaeology and Ethnology, vol. 36, no. 2 (Berkeley: University of California Press, 1935), 170; *The WPA Guide to California* (1939; reprint, New York: Pantheon, 1984), 38.

1. Philip L. Fradkin, *California: The Golden Coast* (New York: Viking, 1974), 8.

2. Frederica Susan Bowcutt, "Wild Restoration: Building Multicultural Partnership in the Sinkyone Wilderness" (PhD diss., University of California, Davis, 1996), 60.

3. J. Smeaton Chase, *California Coast Trails: A Horseback Ride From Mexico to Oregon* (Boston: Houghton Mifflin, 1913), 283–284.

4. A. L. Kroeber, *Handbook of the Indians of California* (Washington, D.C.: Government Printing Office, 1925), 149.

5. Nomland, *Sinkyone Notes,* 166–167.

6. Ray Raphael, *An Everyday History of Somewhere* (Covelo, Calif.: Island, 1980), 98.

THE AGRICULTURAL COAST

Epigraphs: Coast and Geodetic Survey, *United States Coast Pilot, Pacific Coast* (Washington, D.C.: Government Printing Office, 1909), 65; *The WPA Guide to California* (1939; reprint, New York: Pantheon, 1984), 325; Philip L. Fradkin,

California: The Golden Coast (New York: Viking, 1974), 28; National Oceanic and Atmospheric Administration, *United States Coast Pilot, Pacific Coast* (Washington, D.C.: Government Printing Office, 2006), 326.

1. Robert F. Heizer, *Elizabethan California* (Ramona, Calif.: Ballena, 1974), 85, 92.

2. Richard Henry Dana Jr., *Two Years Before the Mast* (New York: Modern Library, 2001), 249.

3. Joseph Warren Revere, *Naval Duty in California* (Oakland, Calif.: Biobooks, 1947), 68.

4. Betty Goerke, *Chief Marin* (Berkeley, Calif.: Heyday, 2007), 165–166.

5. Ibid., 165.

6. D. S. (Dewey) Livingston, *Ranching on the Point Reyes Peninsula* (Point Reyes Station, Calif.: National Park Service, 1993), ix.

7. *History of Marin County, California* (San Francisco: Alley, Bowen & Co., 1880), 136.

8. Ibid., 42.

9. J. Smeaton Chase, *California Coast Trails: A Horseback Ride From Mexico to Oregon* (Boston: Houghton Mifflin, 1913), 249–251.

10. Ibid., 251.

11. Ibid., 252.

12. Ibid., 255.

13. Ibid., 256.

14. Jack Mason, *Point Reyes: The Solemn Land* (Inverness, Calif.: North Shore, 1980), 105.

15. Jack Mason, *Point Reyes West* (Inverness, Calif.: North Shore, 1984), 118.

16. National Park Service, *Staff Report for the Giacomini Ranch Wetlands Restoration Project* (San Francisco, Calif.: Golden Gate National Recreation Area, 1994), 9.

17. Ibid.; Livingston, *Ranching on the Point Reyes Peninsula,* 73.

18. Ellie Rilla, county director, University of California Cooperative Extension, personal interview, June 19, 2008.

THE RESIDENTIAL COAST

Epigraphs: J. Smeaton Chase, *California Coast Trails: A Horseback Ride From Mexico to Oregon* (Boston: Houghton Mifflin, 1913), 239–240; Herbert Eugene Bolton, *Fray Juan Crespi: Missionary Explorer on the Pacific Coast, 1769–1774* (Berkeley: University of California Press, 1927), 226–227; Philip L. Fradkin, *California: The Golden Coast* (New York: Viking, 1974), 27; National Oceanic and Atmospheric Administration, *United States Coast Pilot, Pacific Coast* (Washington, D.C.: Government Printing Office, 2006), 322.

1. Gary Griggs, Kiki Patsch, and Lauret Savoy, *Living with the Changing California Coast* (Berkeley: University of California Press, 2005), 123–124.

2. Holman & Associates, *Archaeological Investigations of the Mussel Rock Site* (San Francisco, Calif.: Holman & Associates, 1986), 52–53.

3. N. J. Lee, "History of Thornton Beach State Park," n.d., mimeographed pamphlet.

4. Earth Investigations Consultants, *Engineering Geologic Evaluation, Bluff Retreat, West Side of Skyline Drive North of Hillview Court, Daly City, California* (Pacifica, Calif.: Earth Investigations Consultants, 2004), 1.

5. Cotton, Shires & Associates, *Geotechnical Report: Northridge Bluff Landslide* (Los Gatos, Calif.: Cotton, Shires & Associates, 2004), 26.

6. State Earthquake Investigation Commission, *The California Earthquake of April 18, 1906* (Washington, D.C.: Carnegie Institution of Washington, 1908), 92.

7. "Geology of Mussel Rock Landslide," *California Geology* 40 (March 1987): 65.

8. Ibid., 10–11.

9. Rasa Gustaitis, "Lines in the Sand," *California Coast & Ocean* (Spring 1998): 2.

THE TOURIST COAST

Epigraphs: Richard Henry Dana Jr., *Two Years Before the Mast* (1840; reprint, New York: Modern Library, 2001), 89; Coast and Geodetic Survey, *United States Coast Pilot, Pacific Coast* (Washington, D.C.: Government Printing Office, 1909), 64; J. Smeaton Chase, *California Coast Trails: A Horseback Ride From Mexico to Oregon* (Boston: Houghton Mifflin, 1913), 219; *The WPA Guide to California* (1939; reprint, New York: Pantheon, 1984), 232–233; Philip L. Fradkin, *California: The Golden Coast* (New York: Viking, 1974), 30.

1. Robert Louis Stevenson, "The Old Pacific Capital," in *The Lantern Bearers and Other Essays*, ed. Jeremy Treglown (New York: Farrar, Straus and Giroux, 1988), 127, 131, 135, 136, 138.

2. Ibid., 131.

3. Connie Young Chiang, "Shaping the Shoreline Environment, Society, and Culture in Monterey, California" (PhD diss., Department of History, University of Washington, Seattle, 2002), 42, 54, 56.

4. John Steinbeck, *Tortilla Flat* (New York: Viking Penguin, 1986), 169.

5. Tom Mangelsdorf, *A History of Steinbeck's Cannery Row* (Santa Cruz, Calif.: Western Tanager, 1986), 25.

6. Ibid., 39.

7. Carroll W. Pursell Jr., "The History and Significance of the Hovden Cannery" (Monterey, Calif.: Monterey Bay Aquarium Foundation, 1979), 22.

8. Eric Enno Tamm, *Beyond the Outer Shores* (New York: Four Walls Eight Windows, 2004), 91.

9. Ibid., 283.

10. "Cannery Row at 50: Turning Silver Into Gold," *Via*, May–June 2008, A10.

11. "Economic Impact Study Finds Nonprofit Aquarium Contributes $250 Million a Year to State's Economy," news release, Monterey Bay Aquarium, Monterey, Calif., December 12, 2004.

12. *Monterey Bay Aquarium: The Insider's Guide* (Monterey, Calif.: Monterey Bay Aquarium, 2005), 2.

THE RECREATIONAL COAST

Epigraphs: Coast and Geodetic Survey, *United States Coast Pilot, Pacific Coast* (Washington, D.C.: Government Printing Office, 1909), 47; *The WPA Guide to California* (1939; reprint, New York: Pantheon, 1984), 417; National Oceanic and Atmospheric Administration, *United States Coast Pilot, Pacific Coast* (Washington, D.C.: Government Printing Office, 2006), 283.

1. J. Smeaton Chase, *California Coast Trails: A Horseback Ride From Mexico to Oregon* (Boston: Houghton Mifflin, 1913), 55.

2. Richard Henry Dana Jr., *Two Years Before the Mast* (New York: Modern Library, 2001), 75.

3. National Oceanic and Atmospheric Administration, *United States Coast Pilot*, 291.

4. Carey McWilliams, *Southern California: An Island On the Land* (Salt Lake City: Peregrine Smith, 1988), 7.

5. Suzan Given et al., "Regional Public Health Cost Estimates of Contaminated Coastal Waters: A Case Study of Gastroenteritis at Southern California Beaches," *Environmental Science & Technology* 40 (September–October 2006): 4851–4858.

6. The source for all quotes about the Santa Monica Pier, unless otherwise noted, is a thick compendium of stories from the *Santa Monica Outlook* and *Los Angeles Times* dating from 1875 to 1990 and compiled by Santa Monica Pier historian Jim Harris.

7. Reyner Banham, "The Historian on the Pier," *New Society* 17 (January 14, 1971): 67.

8. Mike Grimmer and Hallie Jones, "What's Up with the Pier?" *Currents*, Winter 2006, 6.

9. "L.A. County Diverts Marina del Rey Revenue to Balance Budget for Year," *Los Angeles Business Journal*, May 31, 1993; "Welcome Wave at the Marina," *Los Angeles Times*, April 17, 1997.

10. Jack London, *The Cruise of the Snark* (London: Seafarer Books, 1971), 87.

11. "Lifeguard History: 1900's," n.d., County of Los Angeles Lifeguard Division, www.fire.lacounty.gov/Lifeguards/WhoIsHistoryByDecade.asp, accessed August 6, 2008.

THE INDUSTRIAL COAST

Epigraphs: Richard Henry Dana Jr., *Two Years Before the Mast* (1840; reprint, New York: Modern Library, 2001), 105; Coast and Geodetic Survey, *United States Coast Pilot, Pacific Coast* (Washington, D.C.: Government Printing Office, 1909), 44; Philip L. Fradkin, *California: The Golden Coast* (New York: Viking, 1974), 96; National Oceanic and Atmospheric Administration, *United States Coast Pilot, Pacific Coast* (Washington, D.C.: Government Printing Office, 2006), 269.

1. Port of Los Angeles, www.portoflosangeles.org/newsroom/press_kit/facts.asp.

2. Captain Amos A. Fries, "San Pedro Harbor," *Out West* 27 (October 1907): 311.

3. Dana, *Two Years Before the Mast*, 116, 277.

4. James S. Cannon, "U.S. Container Ports and Air Pollution: A Perfect Storm" (Boulder, Colo.: Energy Futures, 2008), 7.

THE MILITARY COAST

Epigraphs: Richard Henry Dana Jr., *Two Years Before the Mast* (1840; reprint, New York: Modern Library, 2001), 133; Coast and Geodetic Survey, *United States Coast Pilot, Pacific Coast* (Washington, D.C.: Government Printing Office, 1909), 40; J. Smeaton Chase, *California Coast Trails: A Horseback Ride From Mexico to Oregon* (Boston: Houghton Mifflin, 1913), 352; *The WPA Guide to California* (1939; reprint, New York: Pantheon, 1984), 260–261; National Oceanic and Atmospheric Administration, *United States Coast Pilot, Pacific Coast* (Washington, D.C.: Government Printing Office, 2006), 256.

1. Roger W. Lotchin, *Fortress California, 1910–1961* (New York: Oxford University Press, 1992), 297.

2. Harry Kelsey, *Juan Rodríguez Cabrillo* (San Marino, Calif.: Huntington Library, 1998), 143.

3. Lotchin, *Fortress California*, 1.

4. Herbert Eugene Bolton, *Fray Juan Crespí: Missionary Explorer on the Pacific Coast, 1769–1774* (Berkeley: University of California Press, 1927), 2, 118.

5. Dana, *Two Years Before the Mast*, 120.

6. Bruce Linder, *San Diego's Navy: An Illustrated History* (Annapolis, Md.: Naval Institute Press, 2001), 66.

7. Mike Davis, quoted in Mike Davis, Kelly Mayhew, and Jim Miller, eds., *Under the Perfect Sun: The San Diego Tourists Never See* (New York: New Press, 2005), 18, 43.

8. Linder, *San Diego's Navy*, 80.

9. Ibid.; Gary Griggs, Kiki Patsch, and Lauret Savoy, *Living with the Changing California Coast* (Berkeley: University of California Press, 2005), 474.

10. Abraham J. Shragge, "Aircraft Carriers and the Development of San Diego Harbor Since 1930," *Mains'l Haul* 38 (Fall 2002–Winter 2003): 66.

11. "Third Carrier Headed to S.D.," *San Diego Union*, March 30, 2007.

12. M. J. Hameedi, E. R. Long, and M. R. Harman, *Sediment Toxicity in U.S. Coastal Waters* (Silver Spring, Md.: National Oceanic and Atmospheric Administration, 1998), online at http://state-of-coast.noaa.gov/bulletins/html/sed_15sed.html, accessed March 15, 2007.

13. Kelly Mayhew, "Life in Vacationland," in Davis, Mayhew, and Miller, *Under the Perfect Sun,* 331.

14. Joy B. Zedler, Christopher S. Nordby, and Barbara E. Kus, *The Ecology of Tijuana Estuary, California: A National Estuarine Research Reserve* (San Diego: Pacific Estuarine Research Laboratory, Biology Department, San Diego State University, 1992), 5.

15. Ricin can be made from the castor bean into a deadly poison and employed in bioterrorism. The bean grows along the Tijuana River. Ricin is also used as a cancer treatment.

16. U.S. Border Patrol, www.usborderpatrol.com/Border _Patrol1302.htm, accessed August 11, 2010.

17. Kem Nunn, *Tijuana Straits* (New York: Scribner, 2004), 37.

THE POLITICAL COAST

Epigraphs: Coast and Geodetic Survey, *United States Coast Pilot, Pacific Coast* (Washington, D.C.: Government Printing Office, 1909), 44; *The WPA Guide to California* (1939; reprint, New York: Pantheon, 1984), 422; National Oceanic and Atmospheric Administration, *United States Coast Pilot, Pacific Coast* (Washington, D.C.: Government Printing Office, 2006), 267; *Huntington Beach Visitors Guide* (Minneapolis: Tiger Oak Publications for Huntington Beach Conference and Visitors Bureau, 2008), 26.

1. William Morris, "Aera Huntington Beach Field Update," n.d., Society of Petroleum Engineers, Los Angeles Basin Section, www.laspe.org/petrotech/petroFeb08.html, accessed August 11, 2010.

2. James A. Aldridge, ed., *Saving the Bolsa Chica Wetlands* (Fullerton: California State University, Fullerton, Oral History Program, 1998), 141.

3. Ibid., 252.

4. Ibid., 342.

5. Michael Fisher, executive director, *Final Revised Modification and Findings for the Commission's November 29, 1984 Approval of a Land Use Plan for Bolsa Chica* (San Francisco: California Coastal Commission), February 5, 1985.

6. To arrive at the 1,318-acre size of the Bolsa Chica Ecological Reserve, add the 320 acres obtained in the land trade, the 892 acres of wetlands, and the 106 upland acres on the mesa.

SUGGESTED READING

The following sources can be obtained from bookstores, libraries, and the Internet. I've arranged the works under their appropriate headings and in chronological order on the assumption that knowledge builds upon knowledge. What is not listed is the myriad of other books, reports, journal articles, newspaper and magazine stories, Web sites, interviews, memories, and hard-to-find miscellaneous items that made up the bulk of research for this book.

GENERAL

Coast and Geodetic Survey. *United States Coast Pilot, Pacific Coast*. Washington, D.C.: Government Printing Office, 1909.

Chase, J. Smeaton. *California Coast Trails: A Horseback Ride From Mexico to Oregon*. Boston: Houghton Mifflin, 1913.

Watkins, T. H. *On the Shore of the Sundown Sea*. Baltimore: Johns Hopkins University Press, 1973.

Fradkin, Philip L. *California: The Golden Coast*. New York: Viking, 1974.

Bascom, Willard. *Waves and Beaches: The Dynamics of the Ocean Surface*. Garden City, N.Y.: Anchor, 1980.

California Coastal Commission. *California Coastal Resource Guide*. Berkeley: University of California Press, 1987.

Kelsey, Harry. *Juan Rodríguez Cabrillo*. San Marino, Calif.: Huntington Library, 1998.

Paddison, Joshua, ed. *A World Transformed: Firsthand Accounts of California Before the Gold Rush*. Berkeley: Heyday, 1999.

Dana, Richard Henry, Jr. *Two Years Before the Mast*. New York: Modern Library, 2001. First published in 1840.

National Oceanic and Atmospheric Administration. *United States Coast Pilot, Pacific Coast*. Washington, D.C.: Government Printing Office, 2006.

THE WILD COAST

Nomland, Gladys Ayer. *Sinkyone Notes*. University of California Publications in American Archaeology and Ethnology, vol. 36, no. 2. Berkeley: University of California Press, 1935.

Raphael, Ray. *An Everyday History of Somewhere.* Covelo, Calif.: Island Press, 1980.

Evarts, John, and Marjorie Popper, eds. *Coast Redwood: A Natural and Cultural History.* Los Olivos, Calif.: Cachuma, 2001.

Cook, Margarite, and Diane Hawk. *A Glance Back: Northern Mendocino County History.* Piercy, Calif.: Hawk Mountaintop, 2001.

Bureau of Land Management. *King Range National Conservation Area, Proposed Resource Management Plan and Final Environmental Impact Statement,* vols. 1 and 2. Arcata, Calif.: Bureau of Land Management, 2004.

THE AGRICULTURAL COAST

Mason, Jack. *Point Reyes: The Solemn Land.* Inverness, Calif.: North Shore, 1980.

Hart, John. *Farming on the Edge: Saving Family Farms in Marin County, California.* Berkeley: University of California Press, 1991.

Livingston, Dewey. *Ranching on the Point Reyes Peninsula.* Point Reyes Station, Calif.: National Park Service, 1993.

Koehl, Mimi. *Wave-Swept Shore: The Rigors of Life on a Rocky Coast.* Berkeley: University of California Press, 2006.

Goerke, Betty. *Chief Marin.* Berkeley, Calif.: Heyday, 2007.

DeRooy, Carola, and Dewey Livingston. *Point Reyes Peninsula.* San Francisco: Arcadia, 2008.

Livingston, Dewey. *Discovering Historic Ranches at Point Reyes.* Olema, Calif.: Point Reyes National Seashore Association, 2009.

THE RESIDENTIAL COAST

State Earthquake Investigation Commission. *The California Earthquake of April 18, 1906.* Washington, D.C.: Carnegie Institution of Washington, 1908.

Griggs, Gary, Kiki Patsch, and Lauret Savoy. *Living with the Changing California Coast.* Berkeley: University of California Press, 2005.

Smookler, Michael. *San Mateo County Coast.* San Francisco: Arcadia, 2005.

THE TOURIST COAST

Mangelsdorf, Tom. *A History of Steinbeck's Cannery Row.* Santa Cruz, Calif.: Western Tanager, 1986.

Walton, John. *Storied Land: Community and Memory in Monterey.* Berkeley: University of California Press, 2001.

Deans, Nora L., ed. *A Natural History of the Monterey Bay National Marine Sanctuary.* Monterey, Calif.: Monterey Bay Aquarium, 2006.

THE RECREATIONAL COAST

McWilliams, Carey. *Southern California: An Island On the Land.* Salt Lake City: Peregrine Smith, 1988.

Peralta, Stacey, dir. *Dogtown and Z-Boys,* documentary video, 2001.

Alexander, Carolyn Elayne. *Venice.* San Francisco: Arcadia, 2004.

Given, Suzan, et al. "Regional Public Health Cost Estimates of Contaminated Coastal Waters: A Case Study of Gastroenteritis at Southern California Beaches." *Environmental Science & Technology* 40 (September–October, 2006).

Arlington West Memorial, Web site and video, www.arlingtonwestsantamonica.org.

Heal the Bay. Weekly and annual beach reports, www.healthebay.org.

SUGGESTED READING

THE INDUSTRIAL COAST

Economic Survey of the Port of Los Angeles. Los Angeles: Board of Economic Survey, July 15, 1933.

Joe McKinzie, *San Pedro Bay*. San Francisco: Arcadia, 2005.

Marquez, Ernest, and Veronique de Turenne. *Port of Los Angeles: An Illustrated History from 1850 to 1945.* Los Angeles: Port of Los Angeles, 2007.

Mariners Guide. Los Angeles: Port of Los Angeles, 2008.

White, Michael D. *The Port of Los Angeles.* San Francisco: Arcadia, 2008.

America's Port. National Geographic Channel, http://channel.nationalgeographic.com/series/americas-port/all/Overview.

Natural Resources Defense Council and Port of Los Angeles, air quality articles in general, www.nrdc.org and www.portoflosangeles.org.

THE MILITARY COAST

Bolton, Herbert Eugene. *Fray Juan Crespi: Missionary Explorer on the Pacific Coast, 1769–1774.* Berkeley: University of California Press, 1927.

Joy B. Zedler, Christopher S. Nordby, and Barbara E. Kus. *The Ecology of Tijuana Estuary, California: A National Estuarine Research Reserve.* San Diego: Pacific Estuarine Research Laboratory, Biology Department, San Diego State University, 1992.

Lotchin, Roger W. *Fortress California, 1910–1961.* New York: Oxford University Press, 1992.

Joyce, Barry Alan. *A Harbor Worth Defending: A Military History of Point Loma.* San Diego: Cabrillo History Association, 1995.

Linder, Bruce. *San Diego's Navy: An Illustrated History.* Annapolis, Md.: Naval Institute Press, 2001.

Pryde, Philip R. *San Diego: An Introduction to the Region.* San Diego: Sunbelt, 2004.

Nunn, Kem. *Tijuana Straits.* New York: Scribner, 2004.

Davis, Mike, Kelly Mayhew, and Jim Miller, eds. *Under the Perfect Sun: The San Diego Tourists Never See.* New York: New Press, 2005.

THE POLITICAL COAST

James A. Aldridge, ed. *Saving the Bolsa Chica Wetlands.* Fullerton: California State University, Fullerton, Oral History Program, 1998.

INDEX

INDEX

DESIGNER: SANDY DROOKER
TEXT: SCALA 9.5/14
DISPLAY: SCALA SANS
INDEXER: THERESE SHERE
COMPOSITOR: INTEGRATED COMPOSITION SYSTEMS
PREPRESS: EMBASSY GRAPHICS
PRINTED THROUGH: ASIA PACIFIC OFFSET, INC.